GOD'S INVITATION

Meditations on a
Covenant Relationship

Thomas Flowers, SJ

Paulist Press
New York / Mahwah, NJ

Cover design by Sharyn Banks
Book design by Lynn Else

Library of Congress Cataloging-in-Publication Data

Flowers, Thomas.
    God's invitation : meditations on a covenant relationship / Thomas Flowers.
    p. cm.
   ISBN 978-0-8091-4712-0 (alk. paper)
    1. Covenants—Biblical teaching—Meditations. 2. Bible. O.T.—Meditations.
I. Title.
   BS1199.C6F66 2011
   242′.5—dc22

2010033667

Published by Paulist Press
997 Macarthur Boulevard
Mahwah, New Jersey 07430

www.paulistpress.com

Contents

Preface: When I Talk about God

You made us for yourself, Lord, and our hearts are restless until they rest in you.

—St. Augustine of Hippo

Credo

If you made us for yourself,
You truly are a fool,

For you let us choose,
And hearts designed
To burn for love
Have hardly stopped us

From choosing
Whatever else we can,
Out of stubbornness
And envy,
Though you opened
To us your every treasury.

And still you said
These are my children,
Still you said,
I love them.

And so you came
To share with us
What made us
Unlike you.

So you died.
So you rose.
Still we know
How to be unimpressed,

And so you are a fool,
Which is, of course,
Why I love you.

When I talk about God, I sometimes still get nervous. I have been a catechist and a high school theology teacher; I am a religious poet and a Jesuit: people expect me to talk about God. And I love to do it. But when I talk about God, I am exposing my heart and when I think about that too much, it scares me—because I love the Lord, and my relationship with God is not an abstract, but a concrete part of my daily life. And the Lord whom I love is the same Lord whom Moses and Abraham, whom Hannah and David, knew and loved. The God of the Old Testament is sometimes mistakenly characterized as impersonal, but there is little evidence for this in the scriptures. The relationship of God with Miriam or Eve or Noah is as real and concrete as any human relationship—if it is not indeed more so. This is a book about God: the God I know, the God whom Israel knew, the God who longs to be known ever more deeply.

To know and love God deeply—to be in real relationship with the Lord—seems to require more than piety. Indeed, if we are to take people's relationships with God in the Old Testament as our starting point, it almost seems as if impiety is necessary. In the scriptures, people do not simply pray to God: they talk with God, and even talk back to God, with sometimes startling familiarity. It is tantalizingly intimate and invites us into deeper relationship with the Lord, even as it leaves us wondering where to begin. The Old Testament, in particular, is problematic because so many of its stories perplex us with the odd sensibilities of their ancient authors or the assumed knowledge of Judaism we usually lack. But the Old Testament has the potential to enliven and reassure us, to challenge our assumptions and incite us to greater boldness in our relationship with God. This book brings the stories of the Old Testament into our lives today. It places biblical characters and events alongside contemporary experience in meditations that delve into the mystery of the creator God who desires to know and be known by all people. Thus, it is an invitation to grow in relationship with God through the scriptures.

The book is comprised of five chapters, each of which explores one of the great covenants God made with the people of Israel in the Old Testament. Each chapter contains a series of meditations upon the covenant, and each meditation includes a short passage of scripture, an essay, and a poetic reflection. The scripture passage calls to mind the actions of God and his people in the living out of the covenant. The essay personalizes the scripture by relating the biblical story to experiences from my own life and thus serves as an entry point into the Old Testament story, a way in which you can discover how the biblical account touches your life. The poetic reflection affords you the opportunity to pause and meditate upon the movements of God's Spirit and your own in reflecting upon the covenant. For the covenants of God in the Old Testament were more than the promises of God to care for his people: they were God's promises to enter into true and loving relationship with his people. Meditating upon that covenant relationship thus allows us to consider our own relationship with God.

Each chapter concludes with a guide for further reflection. The guide offers supplementary material to accompany each meditation and is intended as a resource for those seeking further ways to explore the scripture and the themes to which I have made reference in the meditations. For those looking to delve more deeply into the scripture itself, the appropriate scripture citations are provided for each meditation. I have also provided a reflection question for each meditation that can be used as a starting point for journaling, meditation, or discussion. It might be nice to read the book with a Bible or a journal, or both, handy, and to flip to "For Further Reflection" when a particular meditation really resonates with you. Or you might read the meditations straight through and then use the guides as a way to come back to the ones to which you feel drawn. Feel free to use or not use the guides in whole or in part. Finally, for those who might wish to use these meditations as a supplement to weekly reflection on the Sunday readings at church—in individual prayer or as part of an ongoing faith-sharing group, prayer gathering, or Bible study—there is also an appendix in the back of the book that offers suggestions as to which Sundays or holydays in the Catholic liturgical year have an appropriate connection.

One of the great gifts of the Bible is its stories, stories that are truly a mixture of the human and the divine. If we stop at the pages of the scriptures, if we look upon the people and events in the Old Testament as no more than lessons we can learn from or great metaphors, then we miss the reality of how God has loved, and still loves, his people. This book is about bringing the scriptures to life; thus, it can be used in personal prayer, on retreat, in faith sharing, or in Bible study. It is intended as a place to begin: to begin to appreciate the Old Testament more, to begin a deeper relationship with God, or simply to begin yet another conversation with the Lord.

Finally, allow me to make one note about my approach. When I talk about God in this book, I am very familiar in my style. I make jokes, I get exasperated, I gush, I theorize, and more than anything else, I tell stories. I think that the stories I tell say something about who God is, and they reflect my own relationship with God, God's relationship with me, and the love story between God and his first chosen people, Israel. Because the God I speak of is personal, I have opted to use the convention of referring to the Lord with the masculine pronoun. I do not want to be misunderstood: I call God "he" because it is too impersonal continually to refer to the Lord with titles. I could just as easily call God "she," but I do not. Further, the stories I tell, while based in reality, are for the purpose of enabling meditation. Some of it is the story of Israel, and some of it is drawn from my own life. But it is neither memoir nor history, neither fiction nor overly concerned with facts. When I talk about God, I am talking about my friend and master, and so I feel great freedom; but my words and my stories will, nonetheless, always be inadequate.

Introduction:
Christian Character and Faith

[Jesus said:] "When you are praying, do not heap up empty phrases as the Gentiles do; for they think that they will be heard because of their many words. Do not be like them, for your Father knows what you need before you ask him."

—Matthew 6:7–8

How to Pray

This morning I spoke of nothing
To God and called it prayer,
Rambling and complaining,
Caught in my petty cares.

And as my heart grew emptier,
The Lord entered
Through the front door
And made himself at home

Until we were sitting there—
I on the sofa, God in a chair—
And I was at ease,
No more than myself in God's presence.

Which is all I know to say
About how we ought to pray,
And also that when you're ready,
Or not, God will do the talking.

In the beginning, I had no idea what "Christian Character and Faith" meant. I graduated from college with a degree in history. My specialty was church history of Reformation Europe, and I had taken only three religious studies courses. I was, admittedly, a six-year veteran of teaching catechism to prepare teenagers and young adults for the sacrament of confirmation. Nevertheless, it seems odd that these credentials were enough to garner me a full-time teaching position at a Catholic high school teaching classes on the Old and New Testaments and church history. More puzzling, though, than why I was hired was the curriculum I inherited. According to every official document, the freshman course was called "Christian Character and Faith." This was in contrast to what I had been told when hired: then, the vice-principal had informed me that it was called "Introduction to the Hebrew Scriptures." The latter title fit the course better, since the textbook covered the Old Testament and there was nothing in the previous year's syllabus that indicated teaching anything resembling an introduction to Catholic Christianity, which is what I assumed the course title implied. So I wasn't sure how to teach "Christian Character and Faith" through a course on the Old Testament, nor why I was teaching the Old Testament to a class full of students who really needed an introduction to Catholic Christianity.

It would be overly dramatic—and a trifle presumptuous—to suggest that this was the same sort of situation Abraham faced when he set out for the land that would become Israel, but I will say this: we were both lost and more than a little confused. Still less did my first lesson plans resemble the heavens and earth as God first created them, but that was where I began the course regardless. It seemed fitting enough, though, because as I see it, creation begins with foolishness. So I began by teaching my students that the usual rules did not apply where scripture was concerned. There are, I showed them, two accounts of creation, which cannot be reconciled without complicated mental gymnastics and which, even then, hardly explain everything. It wasn't history nor could we simply evaluate it as piece of literature; simple classifications and analyses were of little use. So, I began by descending us into chaos, fool that I am.

Yet foolishness was appropriate, since the God I believe in could also be called a fool. I think St. Augustine put it well: "You made us for yourself, Lord, and our hearts are restless until they rest in you." It is a beautiful sentiment, and one that resonates with my experience of God. But if it is true that we long for God in the deepest part of ourselves, we also ignore that longing well: we are near-experts at doing anything but what will lead us to God, no matter our religious convictions. So Augustine must agree with me that God is a fool: none but a foolish creator would love his creation so much that he would allow it to disregard him.

For good or ill, I built my reputation as a teacher on that sort of foolishness. My students learned quickly that I was rather unflappable when it came to theological complications. At the same time, they were genuinely confused by what I was doing: this was not at all the religion class of their Catholic grammar schools, if for no other reason than because there were no collages, and I didn't have a scrap of construction paper in the whole classroom. On top of that, I expected them to think and to comprehend, not merely to journal half-heartedly about their feelings and to parrot back moral platitudes. This was an academic class, I insisted, so I expected them to learn, as unfamiliar as that was to them in a religion class. The problem was that, lacking the authority of the divine, I had a difficult time creating order from the chaos I inherited and to which I contributed. The curriculum as I received it was without any clear sense of direction or purpose: we were supposed to make our way through the textbook, which merely plodded through the Old Testament in excruciating detail. But I didn't have anything better, because I didn't have anything at all. So while I attempted to rock my students out of their pietistic understanding of theology, I was scrambling to find my own way and to create some order that would make the class palatable for both students and teacher.

I suppose that's why God's promises began to draw me in. My world—just recently the ordered atmosphere of my familiar studies in history—had become a mess. It was the story the Old Testament told again and again: following the Lord seems like such a good idea before the journey's begun, before the road gets hard and unfamiliar. Often enough our own failings make it so, but at the same time, it is certainly true that God's ways are not our ways. God didn't promise that all would be sweet and easy, but his promises in the Old Testament—the covenants—usually came not when the Israelites were strong and faithful, but when it felt as if the world was crumbling around them, often because of their own unfaithfulness. The Lord was always there, ready with one more promise, which, in truth, was always the same promise: return to me, and you will be my people and I will be your God.

I wasn't teaching about an abstract deity, or even about the mythology of an ancient people: I was talking about God. That is what made me unflappable in class, and why the covenants offered me the solution I sought: this was something I knew well. I knew the Old Testament itself, but I was no expert. I had taken one college-level course on the Old Testament that had gone no further than the book of Kings. Otherwise, my knowledge was informally accrued: a little from catechism as a child and my religion classes at my Catholic high school, but more from discussions with my parents and from simply paying attention at Mass. In part, I was learning my curriculum as I went. While I knew enough to teach my class about how Catholics read the scripture and to explain about the two accounts of creation, I certainly didn't know the origin of the feast of Purim or when the prophet Ezekiel wrote before I read it in the very textbook I assigned to my students. My expertise was limited.

However, I wasn't attempting to make my students into biblical experts. I was trying to help familiarize them with the Bible and with how to read and approach the Bible as intelligent, informed persons. I wanted them to know the story and how we, as Catholics, understand the scriptures. I wanted them, more simply, to feel comfortable with the Bible in their hands, at ease with looking up a passage without using a table of contents, and familiar with the breadth of perspectives on God explored in the Bible. Beneath these technical skills were the covenants. I was teaching an academic course and only tested them on their knowledge of the material, but at the same time, I was trying to teach them about God. I wanted them to know the God who made such promises, who saved his people again and again in the face of their own infidelities.

I wanted them to know the God I talk to every morning. It was the odd reality of teaching: I didn't just care about my subject because it was my job—this was my life. The morning I began my unit on the psalms, I prayed, as I did every day, the Liturgy of the Hours—forming on my lips as prayer the very words I'd teach about that day. When I talked about Jeremiah, I was speaking of the friend with whom I'd journeyed through one Lent a few years before. And though I was quite familiar with high school freshmen by the time I taught about Hosea, I simply didn't understand why my students were not touched by God's plea to return with the Israelites to the desert where their love was new. It was all personal to me. Underneath the academics, I hoped to com-

municate to at least a few of them that salvation history was their
history, too.

I don't know if I succeeded with many of them, but I had an
effect upon me. When I began teaching, I already had a few Old
Testament friends: Jeremiah, as I mentioned; Samuel, with whom
I'd learned to hear the Lord calling; Abraham, who never failed to
make me laugh when I heard him bargain God down on the
number of good people it would take to save Sodom (Gen
18:16–33). There were others as well, but as the months passed in
the company of Israel and God, my love for the Old Testament
grew: for the history and the miracles, for the kings and the
prophets, for the promises of God and the prayers of his people.

Amid that greater affection, the Old Testament began to seep
even more into my own relationship with the Lord. It was a year
when a great deal was happening all at once for me. As if being a
first-year teacher was not enough, I was also taking graduate
courses in theology, I had just signed the contract for my first book,
and I was applying to the Society of Jesus. It was hardly a restful
year, although that had been my intention in returning to the Bay
Area after four years in Santa Barbara. My years at the University of
California, Santa Barbara, had been difficult, but they had also been
the most prolific years for my poetry—so prolific that I felt completely burned out as a poet by the time I graduated. Thus, as my
life was quickly complicated by so many different commitments, I
stopped writing poetry: I was tired of my own voice and the effort
it took to find the next metaphor and the next rightly turned verse.
I was not quite Noah in his five-hundredth year, but I was very
weary when I began trying to find the Lord anew.

It wasn't that I had ever lost God, but everything was changing. I was applying to enter religious life; I was a teacher more
often than I was a student; I was surrounded by family for the first
time in years; and I wasn't writing anymore. That was no small
matter: poetry had been my customary way of praying in college.

Further, even as I was now a teacher of theology, I was suddenly a Sunday-only Catholic at church—no longer attending daily Mass, and neither involved nor known at the parish I attended. It wasn't by any means bad: everything in my life was actually going rather well. But everything *was* changing, and that meant my relationship with the Lord was as well.

I think it's safe to assume that nearly every prophet God called already had a relationship with the Lord. Perhaps not a friendship, but without at least a passing acquaintance, without some knowledge of who the Lord was, I don't know how they could have recognized his voice when he called, or could have even heard it without dismissing it outright. The Old Testament, despite beginning with the creation of the universe, has a way of starting in the middle of things. We rarely hear of prophets growing up and slowly getting to know God. Perhaps that's because more often than not we're already on the road when we finally realize the Lord has called us to follow.

So as I spent my days crafting a course around five Old Testament covenants, working on how to weave the theme of salvation history into every bit of the class and how to make the stories of the Bible lively and interesting for my students, my teaching was entering into how I prayed. The Lord and I talk with some frequency. Nowadays we chat, rather informally, just after I get up, before too much else has time to happen. When I was in college, we used to walk along the Santa Barbara coast, sometimes singing together, sometimes in silent companionship. And when I was teaching high school, we tended to talk in the evenings in my end-of-the-day exhaustion. Regardless of how and when we talk, whenever we do, it's a conversation. I speak and God speaks; I interrupt the Lord; I roll my eyes; I wink and laugh; and I sit enraptured. In turn, God cuts me off; God sighs and grins; God listens intently. We do not always talk piously: we talk honestly. Or rather, God is always honest, and whenever I am not, our conversations become quiet and awkward.

In my grand presumptuousness, I tend to decide what we talk about first. I am, at times, not unlike David explaining excitedly to the Lord how he is going to build a temple for the Ark of the Covenant—the Lord listens patiently and then informs me, as he did David, of what we are actually going to do (2 Sam 7:1–17). I do occasionally have a good idea, and when I do, the Lord is very solicitous; after all, God did listen to Abraham about Sodom. It is all part of the dynamic, because prayer is, finally, about the maintenance of a relationship. Halfway through my year of teaching about the Old Testament, I had a very good idea: I started writing poems again. As the year wound on, I began to feel that God was speaking rather rapidly to me and that I needed a way to respond. So the Lord and I slipped back into an old habit. I had been away long enough, and while my verse at first felt clumsy, it never felt unfamiliar. It was as if I had come home after six months away: greeted with the usual surroundings, things looked strange because they were unchanged.

That was not, however, a long-lived state of affairs. Soon enough, I was back where I had been six months before with a noticeable difference: it felt wonderful to write this time. I picked up where I had left off, but without any of the weariness. I attribute that to the Lord's kindness, because my verse became once again central to my spiritual life. For all the familiarity of the process, it was the newness of my surroundings that occupied my poems. Poetry became a way to explore how I felt about all that was changing in my life and to gain some sense of perspective. That it would be was clear from the beginning, as I wrote my first new poems while I was visiting the Jesuit novitiate that I would enter in August 2007. This was December 2006, and I had just been accepted by the California Province of the Society. As part of the application process, I was asked to schedule a three- to four-day visit to the novitiate. I had scheduled the visit for my school break, not knowing I would already be accepted by then. So when I arrived, it was with a clear sense that this was my future, and as I sat in a novice bedroom one night, I decided to write a poem. One was all it took to make me realize how much I wanted to write again. The overwhelming novelty, and foolishness, of what lay before me brought me back to that familiar place where I worked out unfamiliarity.

I was like Abraham wandering toward Palestine. I was pondering the foolishness of creation and trusting in God's promise. The Old Testament was on my mind and in my heart, and so it found its way into my poems. As I struggled with a thousand fears and dreams in the poems I wrote that year, I also thought about God's promises and began a series of poems on the five covenants of the Old Testament I was teaching my students about. By the time I started writing the poems, the Old Testament had grown familiar to me, and it seemed natural to talk about God in that way, to walk alongside the prophets and kings and people of Israel.

I reflected on Noah and the promise God left in the beauty of creation. I pondered the endless love of God and the power of Abraham's *yes*. I thought about the power of the Lord's words as he spoke to Moses on Sinai. I wondered at what God had in mind for David's kingdom. I attempted to fathom a covenant written on our hearts. They were not poems about the perfection of God's plan. God's plan *is* perfect, but not only is it made for flawed people, it seems God's perfection is much messier than anything we would imagine. For God bases it on relationships, not laws; people, not ideas; life, not scenarios.

I wanted my students to understand something of this messiness, and what this had to do with real life. When I began teaching my course in the second semester with new students, I shifted around my syllabus to give us an extra week at the very beginning. I was still convinced that these freshmen needed an introductory course on Christianity before leaping into the Old Testament, and while I couldn't comprehensively rewrite the course, I decided I could teach a week on the Nicene Creed before moving on to the main course material. As part of this small unit, I assigned a paper that I entitled the "Personal Faith Statement." The idea was simple: after studying the basic formula of Christian belief, I wanted my students to tell me what they believed and how it differed—or did not differ—from the Nicene Creed. It was perhaps the closest I ever came to asking them to talk about their feelings, although, in my own defense, the comparison to the Creed was essential, and I graded them on the mechanics of their essay as well. My aim was to get my students thinking about what this seemingly abstract and certainly ancient material we were studying had to do with their own lives. Faith, I implied, was as real as why they decided to get out of bed in the morning. I didn't grade the essays based on *what* they believed, but I did give poor marks to those students who didn't tell me anything they believed. One student spent his essay explaining why religion was not only absurd, but also dangerous. I insisted, in my comments, that this was a perfectly legitimate position to have, but had nothing to do with the assignment. I wanted to know what he did believe, not what he didn't. I wanted to know what made him come to school every day and listen to me, even though he disagreed with nearly everything I said. His answer to that question would no doubt have been messy and not terribly profound—he might have told me something about doing as his parents wanted, or about biding his time until he could leave home and become wealthy and live in as much comfort as possible. That answer would have at least been real, even if it had troubled me on a different level.

It was that engagement with the real questions of life that I desired, for it is what the Old Testament does: it faces the reality, in all its complications, of life in the world God created. Sometimes we all attempt to make it a little too perfect. A perfect argument for why God doesn't exist is, in many respects, a clever way to avoid asking what does exist, what does have meaning. As I wrote with renewed vigor that year, I had to face my own tendencies to gloss over the difficult bits. I had been working for a few years on the finer points of my poetry—on polishing off the rough edges in my meter and language. It was a worthwhile pursuit, but when getting the mechanics of a poem right became more important than what I was saying, there was a problem.

So I wrote a poem with jagged lines and uneven stanzas in breezy, colloquial language. It was wonderful to write, and better than anything I'd written for some time. I started afresh, some-what like Elijah hearing the whisper of the Lord calling him back to the very mess he was fleeing (1 Kings 19:9–15). God called us both back to the reality of what was going on in our relationships with the Lord and his people.

Since then, my poems have dwelt on those real relationships. I have let my poetry ramble only to end up expressing the depths of my confusion. I have told the Lord, "I'm angry at you" and spoken of "your love enveloping me" in the very same poem. I have laughed with God, not knowing what could possibly be so funny. More and more I have found the freedom with God that the prophets and kings and other fools of the Old Testament con-tinually found. It is that freedom that this book is really about. This is not a story about poetry, and certainly not a story about my poetry. It's not a story about me at all. Ironically, it is a story about Christian character and faith.

At least it's about characters and faith. Faith is not, after all, really something we have or don't have. On any given day, we may find believing in the goodness of God or the resurrection of the Lord an easy or a nearly impossible task. Personally, I believe in the mercy of the Lord much better at 6:00 a.m. Tuesday than 11:00 p.m. Friday; perhaps for some it's the other way around. But faith is about showing up. Sometimes it means telling God how furious you are and how you don't really believe it's going to work out. Because implied in that declaration, in truth, is our own humility. I've said it thousands of times in a thousand different ways: it's beyond me, Lord, so here. I'm going to go to sleep now; you take over. I'm going for a walk; you fix it. I don't know what I'm supposed to say, so I'm going to be quiet. I love you so much I ache, and you need only say the word and I'll do whatever it is you're asking of me. I love sitting beside you; so I'm just going to sit for awhile.

Because faith means coming to God from wherever we actually are, as the characters we actually are. That is when extraordinary things happen. That's when waters part, when angels stay our hand before we do violence, when God forgives us and gives us even greater responsibility. It's confusing. It's even more confusing than being a history major teaching a theology course on the Old Testament called Christian Character and Faith, but one confusion sometimes leads to another.

II

When I Bring Clouds

Prelude

When I bring clouds over the earth and the bow is seen in the clouds, I will remember my covenant that is between me and you and every living creature of all flesh; and the waters shall never again become a flood to destroy all flesh.

—Genesis 9:14–15

Covenant of Beauty

The rain itself is beautiful
Showering leaves and trickling
Down stems to muddy earth,
And clouds, too, are wondrous
In wisps and twists and swirls,

But still our hearts grow doubtful
At the grim approaching gloom
Of our sinfulness and squalor,
Of our selfish self-assertions
Made manifest in dark storms.

And we wonder, as Noah did—
Knowing how intentions go—

What hope we could ever have
Of earning your unending blessing,
Of avoiding the floods we deserve.

So you promised not only rain
But laid beauty over beauty,
A bow of light itself illuminating
Your creation as if softly saying
Your love is too beautiful to end.

First Meditation: Creation

*In the beginning when God created the heavens and the earth,
the earth was a formless void and darkness covered the face of
the deep, while a wind from God swept over the face of the
waters. Then God said, "Let there be light"; and there was
light. And God saw that the light was good; and God
separated the light from the darkness.*

—Genesis 1:1–4

I have told God nearly every plan I've ever made, and never once
caught him laughing as I did. I've heard God laugh at my jokes
and even looked over to see him laughing at the worries we both
know are pointless. God, in my experience, is playful and witty,
but it's absurd to think that he delights in deriding our sincere
intentions, as the familiar saying "If you want to make God laugh,
tell him your plans" implies. God would sooner laugh at his own
plans than ours. In January of my senior year in college, my vision
of the year after my graduation looked wildly different from what
actually came to pass. None of the plans I so painstakingly made
then remained unaltered six months later. Yet I cannot imagine

that God laughed at what I prepared, if for no other reason than that I can clearly remember the Lord working beside me through those months. When God laughs, it is always filled with delight in what he creates, and thus it is always encouraging.

I love that Genesis begins in darkness. Although the biblical author is describing how God creates, there is something so human about how the moment before creation is described: over a dark and frightening abyss, God's spirit is on the move. That, I think, is where most dreams begin: in the hopeful dark, filled with fear and confusion, but also with our awareness that God is preparing something beautiful. God was not lost or confused before he created the heavens and the earth, but we are justifiably bewildered in trying to imagine that moment before God loved us enough to create. Each time we come to those moments before creation we, of necessity, rely on hope to get us through. When I was in college, I did a lot of hoping. Reading back over the poems I wrote in those years, I find a lot of beautiful lines and many appealing poems, but I am startled, sometimes, at all that I worried over, all that left me troubled and bewildered. Yet through that confusion and so many worries, I returned, time and again, to the theme of hope. I couldn't see what came next, but I could feel that "a wind from God swept over the face of the waters," so I hoped.

Watching the Moon

I could watch the clock
Torment me with regularity,
As the minutes fall uniformly into the past,
And pray that sometime soon
I'll see the right numbers on the face.

But tonight, I'll watch the moon
And let the sky, in endlessness, surround me,
As the stars look on with sympathetic eyes

And the wind sighs my sighs for me
And whispers of rest to come.

I'll watch the moon
Because sometimes the moon is smiling
Reassuringly down at me
Across the confusing wonderland of the sky,
And I've never seen the same moon twice
As it hangs where it will and reveals itself in bits
Passing the time as the light shines on
An unmappable surface.

I'll watch the moon
Because every night I can find it
As it glimmers on the water
Or washes my treacherous path with light,
Or simply glows,
Almost lost in the sky,
Then I know
That somewhere on the other side of the world
There is still a sun
And a dawn

And this vigil will end
With a bath of light,
Where time and tiredness will disappear.
And until then
I'll be tired, and I'll stay awake waiting:
I'll keep the night
And let the moon
Keep the time.

Second Meditation: The Garden of Eden

So when the woman saw that the tree was good for food, and that it was a delight to the eyes, and that the tree was to be desired to make one wise, she took of its fruit and ate; and she also gave some to her husband, who was with her, and he ate.

—Genesis 3:6

God's delight in creating is evident in Genesis, yet even if it were not written so plainly in scripture, I would assume that God had fun when he made the universe. I'm not denying that it was serious work, but in my experience, there is much to laugh at when God creates. I had thought, before I graduated from college, that I would go on to graduate school. I wasn't interested in continuing my history studies, but instead thought I would study theology in preparation for pastoral work, most likely as a campus minister. I did go on and study theology that next year, but under circumstances very different from any I had imagined. It seemed that as soon as I had my plans in order, the surprises began. First, there was an offer from my brother and his wife to rent a room from them in their new house, and so I had a place to live. Then I sent a résumé, through my brother, to the high school where he worked, looking for a part-time position if something was available; by June, I had been hired as a full-time teacher. Somewhere amid that, my book was accepted for publication, and I decided I was going to apply to the Jesuits. It was a strange time, and I found myself amused at the delightful bewilderment of it all.

My studies were what made the least sense about that year, yet I never seriously considered dropping them. By the time I began my first theology class in the fall, I had no intention of pursuing a degree and there was little time to study amid the work of my first year of teaching. Considering that, it would have been logical not to take any courses at all, but instead I simply lightened the load to one course a quarter. I cannot say that I quite know why I thought taking those classes was so important at the beginning, although I know why I continued the second and third quarters. The beginning, though, was at best, illogical—and more accurately, foolish. I've taught so many times that God created the world out of love, and he did. But sometimes even the recognition of the supreme illogic of God's love can forget the fundamental nature of the *choice* that God made, for real love is always a real choice. We too often think that good needs evil, that light needs darkness, or that love needs hate; yet what we believe about God contradicts every one of those propositions: God is good without any evil, light without darkness, love without the slightest trace of hate. In the beginning, the choice that God made was to go entirely outside of himself, to love past the point of his own loveliness. That sort of choice, I think, should inform even the little choices we make, for it tells of the boldness of God, the daring that allows for our existence.

So I chose to study theology part-time along with everything else I was doing. It wasn't an earth-shattering—and certainly not an earth-making—decision. Nevertheless, I am proud of its bold illogic, particularly because it ended up being such an important part of my year. I knew it would be when I set foot on the Santa Clara campus for the first night of my first class. I had already been teaching high school for a month then, and there was something so reassuring about returning to a college campus. Here was something I knew: I was still trying to learn how to be a teacher, but I was comfortable being a student. As I walked down the campus sidewalk toward the student center that evening, I realized how relieved I felt to be there and I knew that this one evening a week would be a perfect break from the chaos of my work. It helped that the first class I took, Christology, was such a delight: I loved the professor and the reading, and found much of what I was learning useful for both my teaching and my spiritual life.

That, at least, was how I felt coming to class, and what I

thought about it most of the week. On Monday nights and Tuesday mornings, though, I had to live with the exhaustion of getting to and from my evening class and of the class itself. Suffice to say, studying at a university some forty miles south of where I worked, and not owning a car, conspired to make for some very short nights. Yet I kept going to class that first quarter and registered for another class in the winter and then a third in the spring. Somehow, the length of Monday night and the weariness of Tuesday at work could not contend with the promise of Monday morning. On Monday morning, I knew that I'd be able to go to class, that I could be a student for a few hours, and that those few hours would substantially improve the rest of my week, even with a little added exhaustion. God can convince me of a great deal in morning light, and the Lord uses that to his advantage and mine. On Monday mornings, God could convince me that going to class would breathe the fresh air I needed into my lungs. Then on Tuesday morning, the Lord could talk me into teaching, simply moving, despite my tired protests.

I really did love going to those classes, and sometimes they were not unlike a walk through paradise. The classes weren't perfect, and I didn't leave all of them enraptured. As I'll discuss shortly, there were many frustrating elements to those evenings, quite apart from being tired. Yet as I imagine walking through the world when it was new, in those mythical moments of the seventh day described in Genesis, my mind dwells on how easy it would be to love God there. Surrounded only by goodness, goodness the Lord made out of love for us, I'd like to believe I wouldn't hesitate to love God deeply in return, at least not so long as I kept my heart and mind in that grateful air. I sometimes still feel that way walking down a sandy ocean path. It is a bit of how I felt in those classes at the best moments. I was, for the evening, given the privilege of beholding God, of examining the wondrous plans of the

Lord for us, in all their depth and beauty. To say the least, I liked what I saw.

There is, though, always a problem with paradise. It doesn't take the book of Genesis long to tell us that. From the majestic descriptions of how God created the world and humanity, Genesis quickly moves to explain what happened to paradise. Yet, despite the alarming speed with which the story moves from pure goodness to the beginning of evil, there is almost an inevitable quality to it. No adult person reading those opening chapters could expect such a state of affairs to last: we know from looking around us that the world is not so simple. Indeed, given human experience, it is not at all surprising that the beginning of the scriptures seeks to explain the origin of death and suffering: what truly shocks us is the idea that the world has not always been this way. That idea, as I have witnessed as both a student and a teacher, unleashes a veritable ocean of anxious, and even angry, questions.

There are two kinds of questions that always seem to arise when we are confronted with the fall from paradise. On the one hand, we question God and the notion that the same all-powerful and gracious God of the first two chapters of Genesis would allow this to happen. On the other hand, we question and blame Adam and Eve for their foolhardiness: if it was not inevitable—if it was not God's fault—that we fell from paradise, then why, we ask, did Adam and Eve have to ruin everything for the rest of us?

One of the most interesting aspects of the theology courses I took at Santa Clara was the composition of the classes in terms of my fellow students. The program was not intended for academics: it was a "pastoral" theology program, geared mostly toward people who were already actively engaged in church ministry, whether professionally or as committed volunteers. The range of academic ability and theological formation was thus broad. In theory, at least we were all committed to our faith and to the Catholic Church, but that did not guarantee much in terms of attitude toward the teachings or the practices of the Church—by which I mean to say that the problem with the classes I took was my fellow students. They were dedicated and wonderful people, but many of them drove me crazy, particularly with their questions, questions that, it seemed to me, had more to do with their spiritual lives than with the subjects of our classes. It is, in the end, what was wrong with paradise, and why it didn't last: because the Lord created humans.

The problem of Eve typifies the difficulty we have with paradise. We never talked specifically about the Garden of Eden or the Fall in any of my classes at Santa Clara, but I came to know my fellow students well enough that I think I know how the discussion would have gone. There would have been those in the class who could not accept the stupidity of Eve in eating that fruit, implying by their consternation that they would never have been so foolish as to disobey God and be thrust from paradise. Then there would be the group who blamed God: why did God create a temptation that no human could withstand? Surely, either God was sadistically toying with his creatures or was using reverse psychology and intended them to eat of the tree. Of course, there would also have been those who questioned the whole story, particularly upset that the fall of humanity, as they saw, was blamed on the woman and not the man. For the truth is, we tend to bring where we are with God to our analysis of such stories: our confusion, our frustration with the Lord, and our bitterness at societal injustice all come out. Poor Eve herself is thrust into the middle of it.

This essay is not, however, the appropriate place to solve our moral and theological problems with paradise, so I will not attempt to do so. Rather, I will merely offer that what happened in the Garden of Eden makes sense to me. I said earlier that I hoped that, confronted with the sheer goodness of creation, I would have a heart filled with gratitude. Yet I know enough about myself to know that it would not be so simple, that it has not been so simple. For the decision of Adam and Eve is the same decision we make. Presented with no logical reason to turn away from the God who only offers us love, we make the choice to do so, merely because we can. I have made that choice more than once in my life. It is an entirely selfish choice, and one that resents that God is our creator, and that we are thus creatures, lesser by definition. We don't always like the implications of that. So, while I am not proud to say it, I feel like I know why Eve did what she did.

Of the Living

If I say I think I know
Why you ate the apple,
Will they think I mean
I think it was okay?

Because I don't feel
Like justifying myself
Or like condemning you—
I've done both enough before.

But I do know
What it means to say
I won't simply because I can,
Or even because it'll hurt
Which means I'm in command,

Because I'm a sinner,
Like you, Eve,
And we are not proud to be—
Though both of us sometimes
Try on such pride—

But I like to think
We also both know
Something of covenants—

Of love that carries through
Our most sinful parts,

For God did not give up on
The mother of the living,
Nor did you give up on living
In God's presence.

Third Meditation: The Flood

*In the six-hundredth year of Noah's life, in the second month,
on the seventeenth day of the month, on that day all the
fountains of the great deep burst forth, and the windows of the
heavens were opened. The rain fell on the earth for forty days
and forty nights.*

—Genesis 7:11–12

My classes at Santa Clara *were* a place to talk about theology and
morality, but so often that was not what dominated our conversations. For even the most learned and nuanced theological explanation of the Fall does not offer an escape from the fundamental
human question that confronts us in that story and so many like
it. My classmates ruined the paradise that those classes at moments
promised because they were human: they couldn't accept paradise
as a free gift. Neither have I been able to do that in my life, for I
too am a sinner, and perhaps I was part of what made those classes
difficult for someone else. In a way, I think that is at least a bit of

what original sin is: we ruin it both for ourselves and for one another. We find ourselves, time and again, both innocent and at fault. Being human is messy.

The Lord and I end up talking about that messiness often enough. I wonder that he hasn't wearied of the conversation, for each time we talk about it, it comes to much the same conclusion. The difficulty I have is that the Lord's affairs on earth are usually so messy. God's reply, almost without fail, is to ask me why I mind that. God doesn't ask without gentleness or understanding, but he is consistent. The glory of God is not an Eden without people; if God had wanted that, God could have had that. Similarly, God did not want us to serve him slavishly, without thought or choice. The result, in this life, is that God's glory is not revealed in the organized, uncomplicated ways so many of us seek. The result is beholding the beauty of God in my Christology class while simultaneously being frustrated at the distracting spiritual problems of my classmates. Partly that is so because God's ways are not our ways, God's thoughts not our thoughts. Partly it is because we are a sinful, disobedient people.

No matter how wondrous or frustrating the night of class, my Monday nights were always followed by my Tuesday mornings. It was simply my routine, but there was always something shocking about the transition from being a student to being a teacher again. Perhaps that was because I found myself a more impressive student than teacher. My students never allowed my thoughts to stray too far from earth: the beauty and poetry of God's vision was rarely very rapturous to a room full of teenagers. Particularly when I was studying Christology, I would sometimes use in my sophomore class what I had learned the previous night in my graduate course. I was teaching New Testament to my sophomores then, so often enough there was a good correlation and I could slip some tidbit into my lesson. I won't say that it didn't work to do this, but there was certainly something lost in the translation. My enthusiasm, while no doubt aiding in the presentation of the material, was hardly infectious.

I actually loved teaching that class of sophomores more than any other. Perhaps teachers are not supposed to have favorite classes, but I did, as I suppose most teachers do. I liked almost all of my students, but as a class, my sophomores just had a certain charm. I had few discipline problems in that class, and I was more able to be at ease with them, comfortable telling jokes and giving them a hard time, ignoring some of the formalities of a high school classroom without neglecting the material we needed to cover. There was a sense, as I taught my sophomores Tuesday morning, that perhaps I wasn't bad at this after all. The glories of God probed Monday night were tempered by both exhaustion and teenage indifference, but I was at least doing something meaningful, and doing it fairly well.

I wonder if that is how Noah felt before his first conversation with the Lord. Certainly, he must have noticed the wickedness around him. Genesis tells us that he was a righteous man, and while the charitableness that accompanies true righteousness may have stopped him from condemning his entire generation, he was undoubtedly bothered by the disregard for God and humanity that surrounded him. Amidst that, though, he was doing his best. We have every reason to believe that he was justifiably proud of his family and at ease with his own relationship with God. Then, into Noah's sincere efforts to serve God in his daily life came a further request from the Lord. To me, the enormity of the project with which God charged Noah pales in comparison to its insanity. After all the Lord's careful work in creating the world, he wanted, apparently, to start over.

I think I have a small notion of how Noah must have felt. It isn't so much the task or its responsibility with which I can relate, as it is the essence of the interchange that occurred between God and Noah. As crazy as the building of the ark may have seemed,

Noah clearly trusted the Lord and believed that what he was doing was right. I don't mean that he didn't doubt or grumble or consider forgetting the whole affair; indeed, I'd like to suggest that he probably did all of those things. But he built the ark. He gathered the animals and his family and set off into the storm. That he might have grown weary, complained, and wished the responsibility of it all away only reveals his humanity, without casting any doubt upon his righteousness. For he did what the Lord asked of him. When, in the second semester of teaching my sophomore class, I came to discover how abysmal the church history half of the course was, I knew I needed to do something about it. I had the expertise, and the sophomores deserved more. Yet I had already been accepted by the Jesuits and informed the principal that I wasn't returning; I had no need or incentive to invest very much in my curriculum. It was, further, an enormous amount of work to demolish and rebuild the course from nothing, enough that it exhausted me to the point that I came down with the worst flu of my life. I was hardly building an ark, but I might as well have been for the looks of consternation I got from some of my fellow teachers. I grumbled throughout, even though I loved what I was creating; perhaps I complained more than Noah, who had much more cause to do so. But I did it. Clearly that was what the Lord asked of me, as the Lord asked Noah to build an ark. They are unequal tasks, but the same God, a God who asks us to follow: not to understand or even to shut up, but rather to accept his invitation in trust.

In Floods

When God asked Noah
To build the ark,
I'm sure Noah was tired—
For five hundred years old
Means that, if nothing else.

And so he probably grumbled
When the joints wouldn't fit,
He probably swore at the sheep
And said he couldn't do it,
He probably woke up to the rain
And felt old, washed away.

And he probably thought
What little good he'd done—
Enough to drain him to the drops—
Was nothing compared with
The pervasive wickedness
That he hadn't stopped.

And yet Noah's goodness,
His tiredness, his reluctant assent
Was all that the Lord asked,

Was all that it took
For God to save the world.

Fourth Meditation:
The Covenant with Noah

*[God said to Noah,] When the bow is in the clouds, I will see
it and remember the everlasting covenant between God and
every living creature of all flesh that is on the earth.... This is
the sign of the covenant that I have established between me
and all flesh that is on the earth.*

—Genesis 9:16–17

One of the problems with teaching is also, I think, a difficulty when building an ark. No matter how hard the task is to accomplish, its seeming insignificance in the face of the problem is alarming. It is so easy to despair of our efforts to improve the world. Yet the story of Noah is not, in the end, about what Noah did to save us: it is about what God did to save us. Noah's response is foundational: without Noah's assent, the Lord could not have accomplished what he did in that way. God is fundamentally unwilling to trample upon our freedom, even to save us. But the story of Noah points to something profound that many of us who have worked in service professions often forget: the beauty of God's love and God's desire for humanity is much greater than any contrary human force. This is what the covenant that God offered to Noah after the flood promises: that God's love is both everlasting and too beautiful for us to ruin. The rainbow is a symbol of that, coming in all its loveliness just after the destruction of the flood.

Some might wonder, after all that I have described of Eden and Noah, whether I take these stories to be literally true. To be honest, it is a question that I am not particularly interested in answering in this essay. I find the stories both compelling and hilarious, touching and absurd, and that, to me, sounds like life. There is a real sense of God's delight throughout the book of Genesis, even with all its oddities and ancient sensibilities. It is not a delight that ignores sin, but rather one that transcends it. That delight pours out from the stories of creation into my own life; I, too, know something of sin, of the glories of creation, of how God enters in and changes everything. Admittedly, it makes me laugh, but not because the laughter covers over my awkward guilt or the sufferings of this life. Rather, I laugh because I can hear God's laughter more clearly than the clamor of sin.

But Laugh

I was going for composed—
Trying to mime the dignified,
Thinking this was the time
For the sober and the serious,

When I lost it in a grin,
Smiling back at him,
Amused at his amusement,
Tickled to realize
I was the punch line
To his joke.

I know
There's sadness here
And reason enough
In failing flesh
And broken thoughts
For bitterness to drown
Out the sweet,

But laughter
Is not a last resort,
Not a fool's solution
To the unsolvable,

Because truly
He and I both
Were laughing
Long before

I thought to compose myself
Or he thought to suffer

Or we could remember the reason
Why our snickering
Was totally inappropriate.

But first we laughed
At life, enjoying absurdity
And every good gift
We needn't take too seriously.

For Further Reflection

Prelude

Genesis 9:14–15   The Covenant of Beauty

What storms in your life seem beyond God's power to calm? How can you allow God to enter into those storms?

First Meditation: Creation

Genesis 1:1—2:4a   The First Account of Creation

When has the Lord transformed darkness into light in your life? How?

Second Meditation: The Garden of Eden

Genesis 2:4b–25   The Second Account of Creation and the Creation of Adam and Eve

Genesis 3:1–24   The Fall of Adam and Eve and the Expulsion from the Garden

What brings you back to God when you have sinned? How do you approach God when you knowingly did something that has made you feel distant from the Lord?

Third Meditation: The Flood

Genesis 6:5–13   God's Decision to Flood the Earth

Genesis 6:14—8:22   Noah and the Flood

Recall a time when God worked some good through you. How did you react when you recognized God's hand at work?

Fourth Meditation: The Covenant with Noah

Genesis 9:1–17   God's Covenant with Noah

Recall a time when laughter came as a welcome relief amid suffering. What was it about the laughter that gave it such healing power?

III

Look Toward Heaven

Prelude

[The LORD*] brought [Abraham] outside and said, "Look
toward heaven and count the stars, if you are able to count
them." Then he said to him, "So shall your descendants be."
And he believed the* LORD*; and the* LORD *reckoned it to him
as righteousness.*

—Genesis 15:5–6

Covenant of Stars

The stars' stubborn infinity,
Melting into black, fading
Amid the blue of morning,
Always spinning, migrating
Across the night's expanse,

Never ceases to awe me
As mumbling, I'm counting
The mistakes of the day or
Perhaps the sins of the age,
Impressed at so much failure

Until I consider the stars
As numberless, as celestial
As when Abraham looked
And saw what one decision,
One right choice could mean—

That the stars are your stars as
Endlessly as you wish them,
And if it is your wish then
One simple *yes* can be more
Than the near infinity of *no*.

Fifth Meditation: The Call of Abram

*Now the LORD said to Abram, "Go from your country and
your kindred and your father's house to the land that I will
show you. I will make of you a great nation, and I will bless
you, and make your name great, so that you will be a blessing.
I will bless those who bless you, and the one who curses you I
will curse; and in you all the families of the earth shall be
blessed." So Abram went, as the LORD had told him; and Lot
went with him. Abram was seventy-five years old when he
departed from Haran.*

—Genesis 12:1–4

I am seldom lost for words, but in Uruguay, I almost always was.
In the summer of my first year as a Jesuit, I lived in Uruguay for
six weeks while taking an intensive Spanish course. We had class
five hours a day, five days a week, and since there were two pro-
fessors who traded off teaching just the three of us novices, saying it was intensive might be putting it mildly. In addition to our

actual instructors, we had a full array of amateur teachers surrounding us most of the time we were outside class, most notably our Uruguayan housemates at the small Jesuit community where we lived. We were immersed in both the language and the culture of Uruguay, and consequently, I often didn't know what to say: I was always either struggling for the right Spanish word or wondering what I wanted to say in the first place. It was a profound, and profoundly frustrating, experience for a lifelong writer who prides himself in his ability to communicate effectively. In that imposed silence the way I related not only to people, but to God, changed, and in that experience was tremendous grace. At the same time, it was a tremendous relief when I got back to Los Angeles; I had never been quite so happy to be in LA.

I wonder what Abraham thought when he first came to Canaan. The scriptures suggest that his departure from his home and kin in Haran was quite unceremonious: the Lord asked him to go, so he went. Then, when he arrived in Canaan, he built an altar to the Lord and began to make a home for himself and his family. We are left with the clear impression that Abraham was eager and willing to do the Lord's will, and I don't doubt that. But I do wonder what he thought as the familiar landscape became more and more foreign and he finally found himself in a place that did not look at all like home. That summer in Uruguay, it was mystifying to me that the stars in the sky were different. I had always known that other stars were visible in the Southern Hemisphere, but even as I gazed at them, I marveled that it was possible that I could be so far from home. I reasoned that they were just as much God's stars as the ones I knew, but it was harder to convince my heart. Abraham knew, as I knew, that he'd come to an unfamiliar place because the Lord had beckoned, but I wonder how it actually felt to arrive. For listening to the Lord's call was only the beginning; after arriving, he faced the more difficult task of figuring out what the call meant.

Más o Menos

The world was more or less
The same place this morning,
More or less the usual beautiful,
The ordinary exotic mix
Of the foreign and familiar

But for where I slept
Beneath the same stars you made
When the earth was new,
The ones I'd never seen,
While never shivering through
The first frost of June,

And I was more or less awestruck—
Slightly terrified, certainly glad—
To find you leading me once more
Into a place less known
But more familiar by the moment

For the ways you reveal yourself,
The footprints you leave
On the road just ahead
Of where my feet fall

And more or less precisely
Where I never thought to find you.

Sixth Meditation: The Promise of Isaac

> *They said to him, "Where is your wife Sarah?" And he said,*
> *"There, in the tent." Then one said, "I will surely return to*
> *you in due season, and your wife Sarah shall have a son."*
> *And Sarah was listening at the tent entrance behind him.*
> *Now Abraham and Sarah were old, advanced in age; it had*
> *ceased to be with Sarah after the manner of women. So Sarah*
> *laughed to herself, saying, "After I have grown old, and my*
> *husband is old, shall I have pleasure?" The LORD said to*
> *Abraham, "Why did Sarah laugh, and say, 'Shall I indeed*
> *bear a child, now that I am old?' Is anything too wonderful for*
> *the LORD?"*
>
> —Genesis 18:9–14a

The first thing the Lord and I had to talk about in Uruguay was how angry I was with him for sending me there. If anyone had asked before I left Los Angeles if I resented going to Uruguay, I would have dismissed the question as absurd. I wasn't thrilled to go, but I was willing: it was part of my formation as a Jesuit, and so it was, at the very least, acceptable. Yet as the first week crept along in Uruguay, I began to notice a disturbing trend in my prayer: nothing happened. I wasn't speaking to the Lord and the Lord, for his part, wasn't replying. I was soldiering through my Spanish classes and adjusting to my new surroundings, and, through my gritted teeth, I thought that was surely enough. But I knew something was wrong and so after a few days, as I sat in the middle of another empty prayer, I stopped and gave myself permission to speak my heart: What, I asked, was the matter? It was my anger that poured out to fill the void. All I did for the remaining forty-five minutes of my morning mediation was yell at God.

I learned in Uruguay something that seems to have come naturally to Abraham and Sarah. They never seemed to have much difficulty speaking frankly with the Lord. Further, they did not

waver in their faithfulness to God, even though they rarely understood what the Lord was asking of them, and consistently insisted
on working out God's plans on their own terms. Somehow, that
worked. Knowing that the Lord had promised them offspring as
numerous as the stars, but also aware that Sarah was past child-
bearing, Abraham and Sarah decided that Abraham should conceive a child with one of their slaves. Not only did the plan wreak
havoc upon the happiness of their home, but it was also obviously
not what the Lord had intended. Yet God did not abandon them:
he continued the slow work of his plan. So the Lord sent mes-
sengers who told Abraham that Sarah would soon conceive a
child, despite her age. When Sarah heard this, she laughed. It is
such a beautifully telling response. On the one hand, it seems to
indicate that Sarah did not trust the Lord's promises, something
for which she was immediately embarrassed: when the Lord's
messenger turned to her, she lamely attempted to deny that she
laughed at all. On the other hand, it speaks of an honesty before
God that is certainly worthy of emulation. When Abraham and
Sarah spoke openly to God, God listened, and even when they
attempted to take over from God, God patiently led them back to
where he wanted them to be. When I stopped pretending that I
was untroubled by being sent to Uruguay, the Lord began to take
care of me, with gentleness and compassion that was embarrass-
ingly tender, coming as it did on the heels of my sullen anger. My
morning meditations in Uruguay became a place where God
nurtured me, without demands, so that I could make it through
days that were extremely challenging. God had merely been waiting for the opportunity.

The difficult part for me to accept—and the cause of my
anger—was not dissimilar to the conundrum that Abraham and
Sarah repeatedly faced. In the abstract, God's plans seem so wonderful, but God does not deal in abstractions. God told Abraham
and Sarah that he wanted to make of their descendants a great

nation, and that sounded great. But nothing about the way in which God executed that plan made any sense to them, because, after all, they knew themselves well, and they knew they weren't the right couple for the task. Most prominently, they were old and childless, but there were a dozen other inadequacies they probably could have told the Lord, if he had ever asked. I thought that learning to live in a foreign culture sounded perfect for a Jesuit in formation: no doubt, it would help form a better minister. So, too, I recognized that knowing Spanish was a nearly invaluable skill for a Jesuit. It was a marvelous plan so long as it didn't have anything to do with me: because actually doing it was uncomfortable.

We had Mass every day in the community before heading off to the university for class. There were usually just five of us there at the small house chapel each morning: three novices, our novice director, and an Uruguayan Jesuit whom I'll call Rafael. I remember well the morning that our novice director was sick and didn't come to Mass; he had been presiding at mass each day, but since he was ill, Rafael graciously celebrated Mass for us. Even when the novice director had been presiding, Mass had been in Spanish, so that was no shock, but when Mass was finished and it was time to go, Rafael began explaining—in Spanish, for he spoke no English—that he would like each of us to contribute a reflection on the gospel we had just heard. I was rather taken aback. I could hardly believe that he was serious; I barely understood him as he asked us to offer our reflections; how could I, with only a few days of Spanish under my belt, be expected to preach?

I preached very badly that day; my reflection was trite and my Spanish was worse. The fact was, as good a student as I was used to being, I was never more than an average student of Spanish. Having to come up with an impromptu reflection that morning, and then knowing that I'd need to prepare something the next morning and any time Rafael presided at Mass angered me. It was not the most mature reaction, but it was how I felt. The plan of learning Spanish in Uruguay seemed like such a good idea for a Jesuit in formation, but not for me. What angered me was not that God devised the plan, but that he included me in it, wholly unequal to the task as I was. Of course, looking back on my stint as a preacher in Uruguay, I can laugh at the absurdity and appreciate the humility of the experience. At the time, I found little humor in it, and wondered what possible good an experience like that could do for me. Yet somehow, amid my frustration the Lord began to tell me, once I was willing to listen, the same thing that he told Abraham and Sarah: actually, it was all tailored to me specifically.

Sarah's Laughter

There are some laughs
I'd love to take back—
The sort of laugh that isn't,
That awkwardly escapes
In a desperate wave,

Maybe like your laugh
That day, Sarah,
When you might have been
Mocking the Lord,
When you might have meant
To scorn God's plans,

But maybe just knew
The Lord was a fool
To trust you,
That the miraculous was more
Than you were prepared for.

Which is why you lied—
Rather lamely—

Because you didn't want God
To think you didn't love him,

And is also why
I can still hear
The laugh you laughed
As you first held Isaac—

The unabashed laughter
Of one forgiven and then some.

Seventh Meditation: The Sacrifice of Isaac

*After these things God tested Abraham. He said to him,
"Abraham!" And he said, "Here I am." He said, "Take your
son, your only son Isaac, whom you love, and go to the land of
Moriah, and offer him there as a burnt-offering on one of the
mountains that I shall show you."*

—Genesis 22:1–2

The heart of the matter, as Abraham could have told me, was
whether I could trust God. When Abraham and Sarah finally had
Isaac, when everything looked as if it might make sense after all,
God asked Abraham to kill his son. It is easy to be swept away by
the shock of the sacrifice of Isaac: even though we know that in
the end God does not allow Isaac to die, it can seem very cruel.
The very thought that God would test Abraham in this way seems
to go against all that we know of God. But if the story of
Abraham's testing disturbs us, who have the benefit of distance
and theological explanations, it must have upset Abraham even
more. This was not only his son and his hopes that God was

threatening: it was God's own promises to Abraham that God seemed willing to cast aside. Everything that Abraham knew of God seemed to be contradicted by that one request, and yet Abraham was willing to comply once more. To suggest that he did so out of blind and unthinking obedience seems to me absurd; the man who fathered Ishmael with one of his slaves as a way to make God's promises come true was not slavish in his relationship with the Lord. But Abraham did trust the Lord, and I would venture that he trusted the Lord for the simple reason that he knew the Lord. Despite never quite understanding, Abraham knew the Lord was a God of love, a God who had Abraham's welfare in mind in all of his decisions. Abraham must have been furious when God asked him to sacrifice Isaac. He must have sworn and stamped his feet and called God crazy, but that didn't stop him from doing as he was asked. The Lord had left no ambiguity: this was what he wanted. Somehow, this was part of God's plan. So Abraham was willing even to sacrifice his son for that.

It was the kind of faith that I learned in Uruguay. Once I had finished screaming at God that day, I was left sitting humbly before him. Being in Uruguay didn't make any more sense than it had before I let my anger show, but the Lord's patience silenced me eventually. He had listened calmly while I yelled, and that, of itself, was humbling, but so was what his silence meant: while the Lord respected my anger, he was not about to agree that there was no good reason for my being there. I knew that, but admitting it meant giving up my self-righteous indignation and beginning the slow process of listening to God. In that way, Uruguay tested my faith: like Abraham, on a much smaller scale, I had been asked by God to do something I thought was crazy, and like Abraham, I found myself somehow willing to proceed anyway.

My favorite story to tell about Uruguay is the tale of the jackrabbit hunt. It is a stretch to attach any particular spiritual import to the absurdity of that night, and yet it holds a symbolic value in my mind precisely because it was so silly and insignificant. We were spending the weekend at a ranch in the countryside outside of Montevideo. We had spent the day with horses and cows and had been treated marvelously by the rancher and his wife. At about 8:15 p.m., we were sitting around the kitchen table and the Uruguayan Jesuit who had brought us there turned to me and my fellow novices and asked if we wanted to go with the ranch hands on a jackrabbit hunt. I smiled politely, turned to the other novices, then turned back and said, of course, *no*. He turned back to me a few minutes later and announced that we would be leaving for the hunt at 9:00 p.m. It was thus that I found myself that midnight sitting in the back of a truck, with a pile of dead and mostly dead jackrabbits in front of me, praying that the hunters would soon run out of bullets and trying to keep my shoes out of the blood running across the bed. I had already witnessed what could only have been a were-rabbit that took six bullets and, in the end, the physical attack of four men to subdue, as well as a supposedly dead rabbit waking up and beginning to climb over the bodies of its dead fellows. To say that I was disturbed by all this would be to understate the point: I was horrified. But I was also strangely amused, if for no other reason than that I kept thinking: this isn't what a man expects when he enters religious life.

As Abraham's hand was stayed by the angel and the relief that the Lord was not taking his son away poured over him, he may not have had the presence of mind to recognize what had just happened. But in time he must have reflected on the depths of his own faith in God. The test had taught him something. I would imagine that Abraham, indeed, marveled that he could have been so faithful, that he had been willing to go that far for the Lord. At the same time, he must have realized something else about his relationship with God: he did know God after all. In the end, Abraham had been proven right, because the Lord had not asked evil of him. God was who Abraham thought he was, and Abraham must have rejoiced to realize it. Knowing something like that changes everything, though, because to know that means that in every situation, no matter how difficult or terrible, Abraham knew the Lord was somehow there, and somehow on his side. So he had to look and listen even more attentively when confronted with suffering and hardship. The Lord, it seemed, had things to teach Abraham.

I don't know how Abraham felt as he walked back down the mountain with his son; I doubt it was much like how I felt that night as I fell into bed after my adventures on the ranch. But I suggest that there was one similarity worth noting: we both had learned something about our commitment to the Lord. I thought God was crazy to bring me to Uruguay, and Abraham must have thought God a fool to want to throw away his own promises. Neither of us was exactly proven wrong, but our relationship with the Lord persisted. It was not so much that we learned how God's plans actually did make perfect sense in the end as that we learned to laugh at the strange ways God moves. I came to understand, as Abraham did on his walk down the mountain, that God had been present all along and there was nothing to fear. But that understanding was coupled with a profound sense that I did not understand God himself; his ways were beyond me, and all I could do was feel relieved and loved. Standing in awe before the Lord is a recognition that God's ways are not our ways, and yet God still chooses to love and care for us. I think the jackrabbit hunt, as silly as it is when placed beside the sacrifice of Isaac, taught me a great deal about awe, for it helped me let go of the carefully constructed order I attempted to place on my life.

The fear of the Lord, the psalmist tells us, is the beginning of wisdom (Ps 111:10; Prov 1:7). For many of us it is an expression charged with negative connotations, but at its most essential, it merely points to what I learned in Uruguay and what Abraham learned when he was asked to sacrifice his son. Before all else, we must allow God to be God, and acknowledge that God knows what we could not possibly know. That is to say, if we want to get anywhere in our relationship with God, we must accept the humility of our own humanity before him: we are not God, and if we love God and believe that God loves us, then that is not a bad thing. On the contrary, it's wonderful. But that fear and awe in God's presence, that humility before the Lord, is only the beginning of wisdom; it is essential, but it is only the first step. Yet the sacrifice of Isaac appears, at first glance, to be nearly the end of the story for Abraham: despite his long life, we hear few stories about him after that point. This seems to me, though, to be very telling. Very little happened in Uruguay after my arguments with the Lord: I studied Spanish and made it through each day, usually exhausted by the time I slept and almost always conscious of just how much longer we had until we returned to California. The silence and the anger of those early prayers were replaced by a quiet and calm that was at once reassuring and easy: the Lord seemed to ask little of me other than to make it through the days. My story, too, seemed to peter out after my grand encounter with God. But, in truth, that initial testing of my faith was only the beginning of the wisdom I learned in Uruguay.

Knowing God

Truthfully,
I think that most of us
Are mostly horrified
To think you'd sacrifice your son
Even if it was God asking.

And then, of course,
We feel guilty,
We feel ashamed
Of our conditional faith.

But Abraham, I don't believe
You knew Isaac would survive,
And I don't doubt
You thought God was crazy
Or that your heart nearly drowned
In your grief,

Which is why I know you knew
That God would never ask evil of you,

Not because
One damn thing he asked
Ever made any sense,
Or because you'd figured out
A theology of absolute good,

But because you knew God,
And knew he knew you,
Knew he loved you
Better than you loved anybody,

So crazy or not
You were going to obey.

Eighth Meditation:
The Covenant with Abraham

No longer shall your name be Abram, but your name shall be Abraham; for I have made you the ancestor of a multitude of nations. I will make you exceedingly fruitful; and I will make nations of you, and kings shall come from you. I will establish my covenant between me and you, and your offspring after you throughout their generations, for an everlasting covenant, to be God to you and to your offspring after you.

—Genesis 17:5–7

For the Lord wanted to teach me to listen. It was a lesson lacking in the sort of drama that makes for a good story, just as the remaining years of Abraham's life were not dramatic enough to garner much attention in the scriptures. Practically speaking, it meant that my days were filled with the effort of paying close attention to the words and people surrounding me to see what I could understand. I was not to run away from the frustration or the difficulty of not understanding, and I had to content myself with not being understood much of the time. This was not a punishment, nor was this the test: the test had ended the moment I became willing to engage in what the Lord was asking of me. So I went to class and went through my days in Uruguay, all the while learning to be vulnerable enough to listen. Talking, for me, can cover over a great deal of my vulnerability, because I know, in English, how to finesse language so that only what I want to share is communicated. Listening, on the other hand, makes me vulnerable to what other people say to me and think about me. I was no longer in control: I was listening.

That vulnerability, of course, came to the forefront in my remaining prayers in Uruguay. There, at least, I was understood. In my prayers, as I indicated above, God was incredibly kind. I felt, in that hour every morning as I tried to prepare myself to face another day of class, that God cherished me. I was embraced and comforted, and given the assurance each day that I was doing enough, that struggling through Spanish and trying to listen was all the Lord asked of me. Or, that day on the ranch, that all I needed to do was laugh and go along with a hunt for jackrabbits in the middle of the night. There was great vulnerability in that, for I had to accept that I was loved when I felt I was doing nothing loveable. It was a powerful lesson about God. At the same time, God knew very well that it was following him that had gotten me into the difficulty I faced in Uruguay: of my own volition, I never would have been in such an uncomfortable and challenging position. It was why I was angry at God in the beginning, but, more importantly, it had a great deal to do with why God took such good care of me. I don't mean to suggest that God doesn't always want to take good care of us, but there was a sense, as God nurtured me those days, that God was reassuring me that what I was doing was all he asked. God had gotten me into the trouble I was in, and God would get me out.

Abraham encountered hardships in God's service that he might have been able to avoid had he stayed at home in Haran. In the land that would become Israel, Abraham had to relearn his relationship with God. He was tested and emerged with a faith deeper than any had ever known, and so I doubt that Abraham regretted his willingness to leave home and follow the Lord. The relative silence with which the scriptures treat Abraham's life after the story of the sacrifice of Isaac indicates to me that Abraham was devoted to God in those final years in an entirely undramatic and yet profound way. He probably still tried to do God's work from time to time and he probably still had an argument or two with the Lord, but it seems that in the end, Abraham must have learned to listen to God well, even as the Lord continued to drive him crazy. The covenant of God with Abraham to make his descendants a great nation more numerous than the stars was founded, simply, upon God's love and Abraham's faith. It was in Abraham's continual willingness to trust in God's actions that God established his relationship with Israel. God was the principal actor, but what he did was possible because he found Abraham ready to trust him.

It was much easier to be grateful for the experiences I'd had in Uruguay after I returned to Los Angeles. Back home, I could own the stories of Uruguay and grin as I recalled my linguistic missteps or delight my friends with stories of odd Uruguayan customs. It strikes me now as hilarious that I had to preach in Spanish when I barely knew the language. I love watching the looks on people's faces as I describe sitting in the back of a pickup truck at midnight with a heap of recently deceased jackrabbits at my feet. The Lord and I had our adventures in Uruguay, but I was never the hero of the story. Even in my comic retellings of those days, there is a pattern: I was thrust into what I did and unable to avoid doing what made me uncomfortable. God was in command, and my role was to respond to the Lord's actions. When I did speak, when I could find the words, I felt very poignantly that the words with which I spoke were not my own. To speak I had to listen, so that I could borrow the words I needed to respond to everything God was saying and doing. So I learned to listen a little more carefully.

Borrowed Words

> *Voy a tratar de hablar*
> *Pero estas palabras no son mías,*
> *Entonces gracias para permitirme*
> *A usar las palabras tuyas,*[1]

> Though I've mangled them
> With my trespassing tongue
> So used to the use of the words
> I've cherished so long,

> But those, too, are your words, Lord,
> If they're more than wasted breath,

---

1. "I'm going to try to speak / But the words aren't mine / So thank you for allowing me / To use your words" (Spanish).

For no matter the language
All words spring from the Word,

Which is why I love them,
Why I'm always trying
To find lovely ones—
For words were made for love.

For Further Reflection

Prelude

Genesis 15:5–6   Covenant of Stars

What one "yes" in your life has meant more than all of your "nos"?

Fifth Meditation: The Call of Abram

Genesis 12:1–8   The Call of Abram and Arrival in Canaan

Recall a time when you found the Lord in a strange or foreign place. How did you come to recognize his footprints?

Sixth Meditation: The Promise of Isaac

Genesis 16:1–6   The Birth of Ishmael

Genesis 18:1–15   The Promise of Isaac; Sarah's Laughter

Genesis 21:1–8   The Birth of Isaac

What "impossible things" has the Lord accomplished in your life? How did you react?

Seventh Meditation: The Sacrifice of Isaac

Genesis 22:1–18   The Sacrifice of Isaac

What about God's plan confuses you? How do you the trust the Lord when you don't understand?

Eighth Meditation: The Covenant with Abraham

Genesis 15:1–6 The Promise of Descendents as Numerous as the Stars

What words do you find the hardest to say to God? What words do you long to hear God say to you?

IV

The Voice of the Lord

Prelude

Now therefore, if you obey my voice and keep my covenant,
you shall be my treasured possession out of all the peoples.
Indeed, the whole earth is mine, but you shall be for me a
priestly kingdom and a holy nation. These are the words that
you shall speak to the Israelites.

—Exodus 19:5–6

Covenant of Words

There are casual words
Whispered and forgotten,
And heated words screamed
And regretted, but then
There are the words you speak

So mindfully, so kindly
That love seeps through
Even the seemingly mundane
To fill our eyes with tears,
Our minds with sweet peace.

And I wonder if Moses
Marveled more at the words

Or that you spoke them
With such deliberation,
With such a clear intention

To demonstrate to us how
We could avoid evil triumphing
By loving you well and joyfully,
All the while trying to explain
How deeply you loved us.

Ninth Meditation: The Egyptian Exile

*After a long time the king of Egypt died. The Israelites
groaned under their slavery, and cried out. Out of the slavery
their cry for help rose up to God. God heard their groaning,
and God remembered his covenant with Abraham, Isaac, and
Jacob. God looked upon the Israelites, and God took notice of
them.*

—Exodus 2:23–25

I never meant to go to Santa Barbara. Even when I was applying
to college; I only added UC Santa Barbara to my list so that I'd
have a third University of California school; at the time, I thought
I'd be going to a Catholic university anyway. But still less did I
intend to go to Santa Barbara when the director of novices first
placed before me the task of discerning the sort of pilgrimage I'd
make in the spring of my first year as a Jesuit. He told us that we
were to pray for what particular grace—what particular gift from
God—we would be seeking as we set out into the world for three
weeks without plans or money, just a one-way bus ticket. The
overall grace of a pilgrimage, he told us, was to learn to rely com-

pletely on the providence of God to take care of our needs, but
we were to look for something more specific and more personal,
and it was on the basis of that grace that we would discern the
starting location for our journey. It takes less than two hours to
get from Los Angeles to Santa Barbara in a car; I could have
walked there and back, and still had plenty of time to spend in
Santa Barbara. So I was more than a little startled when it became
clear to me that the Lord was calling me there.

But God's sense of geography is not ours. It would make
sense, for example, that if the Lord desired Abraham's descendants
to become a great nation in Canaan, he would have kept them
there. Yet as the book of Exodus opens, the Israelites are not only
in Egypt, but they are slaves being oppressed by the government.
It's hard to offer a satisfying explanation for why God chose to
allow the Israelites to get themselves into this position. Neither
could I explain why God had led me back to Santa Barbara when
I arrived on the first day of my pilgrimage. The prayer that had
led me there had been both mystifying and filled with assurance.
As I listened carefully to the promptings of the spirit, I realized
that God was calling me back to the point in my life where I had
been the most uncertain and that I was to look for some new
sense of joy amid that uncertainty. I perceived that there were
wounds from those years of my life that remained unhealed,
although I hardly knew what they were. My discernment was
characterized by its certainty, but not by its clarity. Thus, what I
found confusing was not why I came to Santa Barbara: I came
because God asked me to meet him there. But when I arrived, I
realized I had no idea at all why *God* was waiting for me there. It
was a bit like Egypt in that respect. God could have chosen to
meet the Israelites in Israel, but he didn't. God undoubtedly had
his reasons for that.

Opening Remarks

I could ask what I'm doing here
Until breath and patience give way
And still not find an answer
To alleviate anxiety,

For I know I'm sitting here
Because you sit beside me,
That I've walked all this way
Because you beckoned to me,

And the question, therefore,
Is why you're here,
And as I muster the courage
To ask you that

You're already smiling,
Already delighted,
Already saying you'd love
To show me.

Tenth Meditation: The Infancy of Moses

Now a man from the house of Levi went and married a Levite woman. The woman conceived and bore a son; and when she saw that he was a fine baby, she hid him three months. When she could hide him no longer she got a papyrus basket for him, and plastered it with bitumen and pitch; she put the child in it and placed it among the reeds on the bank of the river. His sister stood at a distance, to see what would happen to him.

—Exodus 2:1–4

While it is certainly true that Exodus is the story of how God saved Israel, God is nevertheless quite unlike the sort of hero we expect. When we think of God saving us, I think we too often imagine the Lord swooping in alone and fixing everything himself. No doubt, God could do that, but he never does. After telling of pharaoh's extreme oppressive measures toward the Israelites— most notably the decision to have every first-born Israelite son slaughtered—the book of Exodus abruptly transitions to the story of one particular family. We, of course, know that this is the beginning of the story of Moses, God's chosen instrument for saving his people. Yet it is worth noticing that there is no indication in the scriptures that the initial saving of Moses from the slaughter of the first-borns is the work of anyone beyond his mother and sister. That is not to suggest that God is in any way absent from the story, but it does demonstrate that God begins, not with his own dramatic entry into the tale, but with the faithful, loving action of one Hebrew family. It is as if God sees in them the perfect place to begin his great work.

Santa Barbara was an opportunity I gave to the Lord both when I went there to study and when I returned on my pilgrimage. There were many factors that went into my decision to attend UC Santa Barbara, but paramount among them was a choice I deliberately made not to go to a Catholic college. Somewhere in the second semester of my senior year of high school, I realized just how easy I had it: I was so comfortable in my faith and in the faith life of the Jesuit Catholic high school I attended, and I realized that if I went to a Jesuit university I could keep traveling along that same trajectory. That, I realized, was no way to deepen my faith; it was a way that I could coast along just as I was. So I decided that I would go to a place where being a faithful Catholic would not be such a given, so that I could learn something about the world and myself. That is to say, I went to UCSB for the sake of my faith. I returned for my pilgrimage not knowing quite why

I was returning, but confident that the matter was essentially the same: the first time, I had opened myself up to the uncertainties of God working in my life according to his own terms instead of my own, and somehow that work was not yet finished. It seemed so silly to make my pilgrimage that personal, that focused on myself, but it was the opportunity God took. When Miriam was sent by her mother to make certain that her brother Moses reached safety, it was not a matter of cosmic, nor even national, importance that preoccupied her. She was watching after her brother, for her sake and the sake of her family. I doubt she could have ever dreamed where such an entirely personal act would end up.

As if purposely to deepen my confusion, I began my pilgrimage at a house in the hills above Santa Barbara that was the home of my history mentor and his wife. I was allowed, before setting off, to arrange the first place I would stay on my trip. Staying with my professor and his wife was not my first choice, and indeed I remember only listing it as a possibility to the novice director as an odd afterthought, a distant fourth choice for where I thought I ought to begin. So I started my pilgrimage utterly bewildered, for I was both convinced that this was where God had led me and certain that this wasn't how a pilgrimage was supposed to go. I remember the conversation that first night at dinner with great clarity. I had only met my professor's wife once before, and I hadn't spoken to my professor but through e-mail since I graduated, but here I was in their house, enjoying their hospitality. When I asked to stay there I had explained to them about the pilgrimage in broad outline, but they had asked little before agreeing. So it was not at all a surprise to me when my professor's wife asked me, somewhere amid the dinner conversation, what my intentions were.

I told her that to answer that question I had to tell them a story, and that by the end of it, I'd know what I was planning to do the next day. It was a bold statement to make, but I was right, and I knew that even then: if God had led me there, God was going to show me my next step through the reactions and words of the two people he had led me to first. So I told them a story they didn't know but that involved them intimately. I told them how I came to UC Santa Barbara, and how I had become a history major, which had everything to do with my professor. I told them what else had been going on in my life during those years and how much my history studies, and my professor's constant encouragement and challenge, had meant to my life. I told them an entirely ordinary story about my life as a college student who loved history and who had found a deeper relationship with God through adversity in Santa Barbara. It was all very interesting for them and for me: they had no idea how much they had meant to my life, nor what had been going on while I had been making my way through my history degree. It was a story about the slow work of God in my life, and how the Lord had met me at every turn, not in earth-shattering, unfamiliar ways, but in the ways I was most ready to meet him.

Among Reeds

I can hear your mother say,
Make certain he's safe,
And not because he was Moses,
Not so that he could save you,
But because he was her son,

Your brother, in need of his sister.
And I wonder what you thought
Those years later when
God was with him
And the waters split and tumbled
At the motion of his hand.

Did you think of watching him
Through reeds to safety,
Not a prophet, or a leader—
Not even *Moses* yet—
Just your little brother?

Because maybe that's why
You sang with him that day,
Of the Lord gloriously triumphant—

For perhaps you saw
Amid the sea and the reeds
Not mere grandeur and power,
Not just waves and dry land,

But the God who loves more,
Who watches and cares more,
More attentively, more kindly,
Than even a sister for her brother.

Eleventh Meditation: The Burning Bush

Moses was keeping the flock of his father-in-law Jethro, the priest of Midian; he led his flock beyond the wilderness, and came to Horeb, the mountain of God. There the angel of the LORD appeared to him in a flame of fire out of a bush; he looked, and the bush was blazing, yet it was not consumed. Then Moses said, "I must turn aside and look at this great sight, and see why the bush is not burned up."

—Exodus 3:1–3

We know little of Moses' life between being saved from death as a baby and the events that began at the burning bush. Really, there are only two stories from those years. We know that he was a fugitive from Egypt: Exodus tells us that Moses, on seeing the beating of an Israelite by an Egyptian, killed the Egyptian. This event, in turn, led to Moses' flight to the land of Midian. In Midian he saved a group of young women from the harassment of some shepherds and, eventually married one of them, becoming a shepherd in the service of her father. There is a similarity between the two stories, for they both show Moses as a man bothered by injustice and unafraid to stand up for the defenseless. Yet in the first case, he commits murder and attempts to cover over the fact; his action, indeed, causes some Israelites, the people he supposedly was defending, to mistrust him and fear his wrath. In the second instance, it is much easier to like Moses, much easier to see in his actions makings of the great man we know. Yet, while murder is no small crime to dismiss easily, these two stories do give us some insight into the slow work of God in the life of Moses. Moses was apparently rash, and zealous in whatever causes he deemed to be righteous. This was the man who encountered God at the burning bush.

Moses responded to the presence of God in the burning bush with remarkable calm and, more importantly, remarkable openness. As soon as he recognized that it was the Lord who addressed him, he called out, "Here I am" and approached the bush with humility. Nothing in his life particularly prepared him for that moment, but God certainly knew Moses well, for he began with the very thing that would pique Moses' interest. After declaring that he was the God of Abraham, Isaac, and Jacob, the Lord told Moses that he had "observed the misery of my people who are in Egypt; I have heard their cry on account of their taskmasters (Exod 3:7)." This was the sort of God Moses' life has prepared him for: a God who loathed injustice and sought to defend the powerless. We can almost imagine Moses slowly raising his head from his hands, his face suddenly filled with amazement and hope. But just as God was winning Moses over, just as the dreams of the man who once killed out of his sense of justice seemed as if they were about to come true, the Lord changed everything by telling him that this would take place not by God's actions alone, but through Moses. Moses' response was to make excuses for why God should not send him, to which God responded by dismissing each excuse. Amid that, Moses asked the Lord for his name, for something to tell the Israelites when they asked who had sent him. The Lord's famous answer was, of course, "I am." It was quite an introduction to the Lord, and one that completely altered the way in which Moses related to God for the rest of his life.

God entered my life just about that dramatically on my pilgrimage. A few days after we had both returned home from our pilgrimages, one of my novice classmates told me that as soon as he set eyes on me for the first time in three weeks he knew that something had happened to me, that something very good had taken place within me on my pilgrimage. There was, however, no burning bush, no plagues, no wandering through the desert or reception of the Law. I didn't climb Mount Sinai or meet God in a tent and walk away with my face shining. It just felt that way. After two days with my professor and his wife, I found myself on the UCSB campus, talking with an old friend of mine from church. I explained to her what I was doing and, more importantly, that I had felt drawn to contact her and wondered if she would be willing to give me a place to stay for a few days. She told me that she was helping to lead a student retreat that weekend and wondered if I might want to come along and help. I knew this retreat well: it was the one I'd always avoided having anything to do with. So without hesitating, I agreed. I dreaded going on that retreat even as I assented, but it was, at the same time, so obviously the work of God that had brought me to that moment. It was not coincidence that I came at that moment to

that person: rather, it was encountering God face to face and recognizing that there was no escape. So I did what the Lord asked.

Divine Introduction

It was all going so well—
Salvation as palpable
As bread on your tongue—

Until the God of the Universe,
The maker of the heavens,
The shaper of earth,
The God of Abraham,
The caller of great men

Said, *Come on,*
I've got a job for you:

For Moses, the criminal,
The husband, the shepherd,
The leaden-tongued uncertain one.

Because suddenly
Moses wasn't sure
Who was talking,
Who would make
Such an invitation,
Or if he meant him at all.

Which is when God said,
Let's try this again,
Because I am and,
For that matter, you are
Precisely who I want,

So come on,
I'll explain as we go.

Twelfth Meditation:
The Covenant with Moses

I am the LORD your God, who brought you out of the land of
Egypt, out of the house of slavery.

—Exodus 20:2

My own brokenness made me fear going on that retreat, and it was in that brokenness that the Lord desired to meet me during my pilgrimage. Moses told God at the burning bush, in so many words, that he felt unequal to being a leader. Perhaps, beyond his stated excuses, he also feared his own rashness and temper; there is nothing quite like the stress of leadership to make flashes of anger a liability. For me, I was afraid of opening my heart and my life to my peers because of how badly burned I'd been when I had done it in the past. I didn't trust the silliness of college students or the openness of retreats because the last time I'd gone against my inclinations and tried to fit into the college lifestyle, I had eventually found myself wounded and uncertain of my own identity. It had hurt tremendously, and I wanted to avoid that pain. I carried the ache of those wounds around with me, and so when God asked me to go on that retreat, it was, I knew, the Lord asking me to drop the weight I carried and approach God's people defenseless. It may not have been unlike approaching the king of Egypt in all his splendor with nothing but a shepherd's staff.

Perhaps the greater similarity with Moses, though, was the knowledge of God's guiding presence. Moses was asked to speak some very hard words, and what he did resulted in the suffering of many. I had to play Ike Turner in a skit and help my rock-and-roll–illiterate fellow retreat leaders with the lyrics to Motown songs. So there were some differences in what we were asked to do. Yet, on my pilgrimage, I eventually found myself shaking the dust from my feet on the city of Ventura, where I was turned away from a Catholic church that had no interest in helping me. Then there were the hard conversations I had to have, and the strange situations I found myself in, like being at a table crowded with Mormons, ex-Mormons, and ex-Catholics. It wasn't quite being asked to predict a deadly plague to the king of Egypt, but there were many uncomfortable, difficult moments for me along the way. What I found throughout all of that was what Moses found: that God was always there with one more idea, one more way to guide and care for me. Cast into unfamiliar roles under harsh conditions, Moses and I encountered the Lord's constant enticement. For God is always trying to win us over, and yet there is nothing sinister about his efforts: God desires our trust so that God can love us more and more deeply. It is what Israel learned, slowly, through the Exodus.

Yet the path God made for the Israelites to walk was perilous. After so many plagues descending upon the land of Egypt that it may well have seemed like the end of the world even to the Israelites, God finally set in motion the escape plan. As the angel of death swept over Egypt, the Israelites, protected by the lamb's blood they smeared on their doorposts, ate quickly and standing, prepared to run as soon as Moses gave the word. It seems to me that it took tremendous faith to be saved by God in the Exodus, for God was always leading them into some more frightful place. The crossing of the Red Sea, while seeming, with the benefit of hindsight, perhaps the most wonderful sign of God's providential love in all the Old Testament, must have been terrifying for the Israelites. That they marveled at the Lord's might I do not doubt, but I can hardly imagine the unease with which they must have walked across a seafloor with water like a wall on either side. To walk that way seems to me a stunning act of faith: for the Israelites who did so put themselves completely in God's hands.

Perhaps I know a little of what that is like. My time spent among college students on my pilgrimage was a time spent in God's hands, for by my will alone I would never have found myself there. I remember sitting among the retreat leaders that first night of the retreat, wondering what in the world I was doing there, scared of what they thought of me and worrying that I shouldn't think so much about what they thought. I learned much about my past and present interactions with my peers on my pilgrimage, and there was much that I was able to heal. As for the Red Sea, it came a little later, when I traveled, on the final leg of my journey, to UCLA. Through prayer, I had decided that UCLA would be the last place I would look for lodging on my pilgrimage, so three days before I was due to return to the novitiate, I presented myself to a group of students who were cooking dinner for a gathering that evening. After the brief awkward silence following my request for a place to stay, the young woman who had the unfortunate task of being the spokesperson for the group began to make excuses. She explained that they were mostly freshmen and lived in the dorms, so perhaps I could ask an upperclassman at dinner that had an apartment. Then a voice chimed in from the back, "Well, I live in the dorms, too, but you can stay with me." It was actually that simple. Before long, he had offered to put me up for three nights and to provide my meals on his meal card at the dining commons. It was a truly bizarre and wondrous experience. It felt a little as if I had walked into a storm and somehow found myself on dry land, safe and warm. I had been positively terrified, and not even that hopeful, as I began to explain my situation to the group, my discomfort and discouragement only growing as I saw the students' expressions darken. But if it was a storm, it was a storm God had led me into, and it was not so much that I avoided the peril of it as that the peril inexplicably turned to salvation. The Israelites did walk into the Red Sea, and I doubt they did it joyfully. But on the other side, there was cause for celebration primarily because of God's saving work, but also because they had trusted the Lord enough to allow him to save them.

Yet after the Israelites had crossed the Red Sea, after the celebration of their salvation had died down, they were faced with the desert—forty years of frustration, of wandering in search of the Promised Land and not finding it. No matter how pious we may pretend to be, I think most of us can understand why the Israelites, from time to time, wavered in their faith while they wandered in the desert. We could speculate endlessly about why they were lost for so long, and blame their sinfulness or question the goodness of the Lord. But if we can look beyond the seeming futility of their wandering, we see not the absence of God in that wilderness, but God's loving presence and concern every step of their journey. It was in the desert, after all, that the Israelites received the Law on Mt. Sinai and built the Ark of the Covenant. In truth, it was in the desert that the slaves of Egypt became the people of Israel. When we read the words of the Law, we too easily focus upon what is human and ancient about it. But the context of the Law is important to remember. The story of the desert reveals to us a God who desired to dwell with his people, who loved his people even when they sinned, who wanted his people to know how to live well and happily. The Law of Israel does not stand apart from human frailties and failings, but nonetheless reveals a God who loved and cared for his people with tenderness and particularity.

I used to joke about just how lost the Israelites must have been to wander for forty years in the tiny stretch of desert between Egypt and Israel; taken literally, the story does seem a little odd. After having made a pilgrimage between Santa Barbara and Los

Angeles, I don't make that joke quite as often as I once did. There was plenty of room for me to wander, and for the Lord to work in the not-many-miles I traversed those three weeks. To say that either I or the Israelites wandered, though, is open to a great deal of misconception. The actions of the Lord in the desert defined the wandering of the Israelites, charging it with purpose; the promptings of God that led me from conversation to conversation and place to place that spring gave every step of my pilgrimage meaning.

I never meant to return to Santa Barbara when I left it for the last time after college because it had been the worst desert of my life, and I was scared to go back to a place with so much pain, so many wounds that still felt fresh. God had not been easy to find in Santa Barbara, and that I had found him during those years was something I was grateful for but not eager to relive. But, after wandering in Santa Barbara and through my past for three weeks, I was able to see things more clearly than I ever had before. Israel first fell in love with God in the desert, and it defined their very existence as a people. I knew the Lord before I came to Santa Barbara, but along the Santa Barbara coast I learned to love God more deeply than I ever had before. I had never been so broken as I was beside that ocean, and God entered into that brokenness, making me more his own than I ever had been. Just as the Israelites could look back on the desert, years later, and see it as the honeymoon of their relationship with God, so I still find myself in prayer, often enough, walking beside the ocean in Santa Barbara with the Lord.

Confidence Man

It's best to be careful with God.
Because just when you've gotten comfortable,
He'll ask if you want tea
And offer you a scone,

While telling you a joke
That makes you ache from laughing.

And eventually he'll ask you
To do something you love to do,
And then he won't even
Blame you when you screw it up,
Holding it, and you, together,
Giving every indication

That he loves you better than you do,
And wishes he could do more for you.
Which he will, if you let him,
That, of course, being his game,
To get you to trust him
So that he can love you more.

For Further Reflection

Prelude

Exodus 19:5–6   The Covenant of Words

What words of the Lord do you particularly treasure? How do you hear the Lord speak those words?

Ninth Meditation: The Egyptian Exile

Exodus 1:8–22   The Oppression of Israel by the Pharaoh

Recall a place where you were surprised to recognize God's presence. How did God reveal himself to you there?

Tenth Meditation: The Infancy of Moses

Exodus 2:1–10   Moses Saved at Birth by His Mother and Sister

What expressions of love in your life best mirror God's love? How can you thank the Lord for that love?

Eleventh Meditation: The Burning Bush

Exodus 2:11–22   Moses Flees Egypt, Saves the Daughters of Jethro, and Marries

Exodus 3:1–22   The Burning Bush

What about the way God calls you confuses you most? How can you bring that confusion to your prayer?

Twelfth Meditation: The Covenant with Moses

Exodus 5:1–9   The First Encounter of Moses with the Pharaoh

Exodus 7:14—10:29   The First Nine Plagues

Exodus 11:1–10   The Tenth Plague

Exodus 14:10–31   The Crossing of the Red Sea

Exodus 15:1–18   Moses Leads the People in a Song of Thanksgiving

Exodus 15:20–21   Miriam Leads a Song of Thanksgiving

Exodus 17:1–7   The Israelites in the Desert—God Provides Water from the Rock

Exodus 19:1–8   The Covenant at Mt. Sinai

Recall a time when you trusted the Lord despite misgivings. What led you to put your trust in God?

V

A Father to Them

Prelude

*When your days are fulfilled and you lie down with your
ancestors, I will raise up your offspring after you, who shall
come forth from your body, and I will establish his kingdom.
He shall build a house for my name, and I will establish the
throne of his kingdom forever. I will be a father to him, and he
shall be a son to me.*

—2 Samuel 7:12–14a

Covenant of Kings

Though our castles may tower,
Ramparts leaning against sky,
Made of bricks that gleam
Blindingly in noonday light,
Showering our land in majesty,

Still time grows nagging fears
As the certainty of security,
The assurance of longevity slip
Into our doubts about whether
There is hope for peace at all.

And it seems David wished
To build a house that would
Promise stability in perpetuity,
With God safely on his side,
Cared for and taking care,

Yet the Lord did not promise
The secure glory of a palace
Built at David's command,
But that the house God built
Would outlast every king.

Thirteenth Meditation: Hannah

There was a certain man of Ramathaim, a Zuphite from the
hill country of Ephraim, whose name was Elkanah son of
Jeroham son of Elihu son of Tohu son of Zuph, an
Ephraimite. He had two wives; the name of one was Hannah,
and the name of the other Peninnah. Peninnah had children,
but Hannah had no children.

—1 Samuel 1:1–2

I could tell that he was dying. It was not because of his age or
health, or even the obvious fact that he lived in a house of the
dying. I was struck, more than anything else, by the way in which
he simply was less present that morning than he had been the day
before. He was still charming and funny, still eating his breakfast
and scrutinizing every detail of the dining room. But I could tell
that something had happened to change him, and I doubt I'll ever
know what it was. Jesuits do not retire, so calling Sacred Heart
Jesuit Center in Los Gatos the retirement home for the California

province is not very helpful, except that it is indeed a home for the ill and aged. But just like anywhere else a Jesuit lives and works, Sacred Heart is a place to which a man is sent and missioned to work, in whatever limited capacity he is capable of working: the most debilitated there are expected nevertheless to pray for the church and the Society. For men used to very active ministerial lives, coming to Sacred Heart can be quite a shock and rather frustrating. Yet what I saw in his face that morning was not anger or frustration, but an evident awareness of death. He told me that he had a secret to share with me, but that it wasn't for the faint of heart. Accustomed to his playfulness, and yet oddly full of trepidation, I told him that I thought I could handle it. So he told me that I was talking to a dead man. Every hair on my neck rose: because I was.

It took me several weeks to admit what bothered me about my work at Sacred Heart, but that conversation was crucial to what I finally realized. I had been assigned to work there for three months at the beginning of my second year as a novice. I was there to accompany the seventy-five men with whom I lived as they died. That, indeed, was the difficulty. Although I *did* plenty of things—wheeled men on walks, helped with exercise classes, led activities—none of it accomplished anything: everyone was still, at the end of the day, dying, and suffering through their days until the last. My presence could not change that and yet my presence was all I had to offer. When that dying Jesuit told me that I was talking to a dead man, I realized that, effectively, I was: his mind and his body were already at least half gone, and it would not be long before the rest of him followed. Yet somehow, in my daily prayers, I did not at first pray about that. It is astonishing to me that I could pretend, even for five minutes, that the eerie weight of the death and suffering around me did not bother me, that the brokenness of the men with whom I spent my days did not make me feel broken as well. But eventually I told the Lord that it drove me crazy that all I could do was watch them die, and in that honest space the words came to me: *It scared me when he said / I was talking to the dead*. So I wrote a poem, and I invited the brokenness of that man, and all the rest of them, into my prayer and my heart; if all I could do was accompany them, then I would accompany them wholeheartedly.

Hannah understood that frankness is always best with the Lord, and she knew more than a little about being broken. Much like Exodus, the book of Samuel begins with a family drama. Hannah, one of Elkanah's two wives, was barren, and felt on a daily basis the shame of that, particularly since the affection her husband showered upon her because of her pitiable condition only served to increase the contempt in which his other wife held her. So Hannah made an appeal to God: if the Lord would grant her a son, she would offer that son for God's service. There was nothing ambiguous about Hannah's prayer or, as it turned out, about the fulfillment of her promise. Hannah's honesty has long impressed me: she knew what she wanted and she asked for it. I think in a way it was her very brokenness that made her so bold. Hannah was undoubtedly a strong and forthright woman in normal circumstances, but it was her reaction to her own suffering that shows us so clearly who she was. Hannah was bitter and angry with the Lord, but she boldly brought that to God instead of sulking in secret, harboring a grudge against the God who had made her barren. It was Hannah's boldness that I learned at Sacred Heart Center.

Simple Complaint

I guess I might say
She lacked subtlety
And not mean it smugly.

Because Hannah knew
What broke her heart
And just what God
Could do to fix it,

And she wasn't afraid
To look a fool or to be one,
To ask the improbable
Or to promise indiscriminately.

Which is to say,
She wasn't asking
For miracles of abstraction,
For divine light that could
Illumine a darkened heart—

She just wanted dignity,
Wanted the joy of a son,
And she lacked the subtlety
To pretend she was happy
Until the Lord listened.

Fourteenth Meditation: King David

*But the thing displeased Samuel when they said, "Give us a
king to govern us." Samuel prayed to the LORD, and the
LORD said to Samuel, "Listen to the voice of the people in all
that they say to you; for they have not rejected you, but they
have rejected me from being king over them."*

—1 Samuel 8:6–7

There was no way to avoid confronting brokenness and suffering at Sacred Heart. Yet it took me two weeks to recognize that, and when I did it was not because of the suffering itself, but because of what happened in my prayer. For the Lord was not waiting for me in my timidity: God desired my boldness and waited for me amid the suffering. It is the paradox we so often encounter in our relationship with the Lord: in those places where God seems most obviously absent, God is even more present. It is what Hannah learned when she asked for a child. The Lord listened to her tearful prayer and healed her of her barrenness so that she might give birth to Samuel. It was Samuel who anointed the first two kings of Israel and effectively inaugurated the kingdom, and I think it is more than coincidence that the history of the kingdom of Israel began in such brokenness. Yet while it is easy to look from a safe distance at a story such as Hannah's and to marvel at the works of the Lord, it is a much more difficult task to face the reality of suffering and brokenness in our own lives and to find God there. For the reality of suffering makes most of us, at some point, question the goodness of the God who allows it and even, apparently, uses it for his own ends. Yet it was my love of God, and my desire to be with God, that bid me enter into that suffering at Sacred Heart.

So I should not have been surprised that encountering the suffering of dying Jesuits was nothing like I supposed it would be. Every morning, I went to breakfast twice. Despite the constant consternation it caused to those with whom I sat at the second meal, I did not actually eat breakfast twice, but I did go to two separate meals: the first upstairs in the main dining room that served for those ambulatory enough to make it to meals on their own, and the second downstairs in the infirmary with the men who needed more individual attention from the nursing staff. The infirmary dining room was a quiet place when I arrived: there were really only two tables where any substantial conversation took place, and even then only intermittently. This was not due to dysfunction in relationships, but rather because of the particular ailments that brought them all together. But they were more capable of conversation, I found, than it first appeared, and for better or for worse, I tended to turn that dining room into a much more raucous place. After normal morning pleasantries, my usual tactic was to be just about as animated and foolish as I could muster at 8:30 a.m.: which for me was quite animated indeed. Very quickly, I fell in love with making them laugh.

One Jesuit in particular, whom I'll call John—because nearly all of them were named either John, Tom, or Dick, even though this man actually wasn't—was a project of mine. I realized without being told that this was man who had once had a delightful sense of humor and must have simply commanded the dinner table in his heyday. He had been smart and quick and loved to point out the absurd. He was also at a very advanced stage of Alzheimer's disease and was thus no longer quick at all and incapable of commanding anything. It should have been sad to see the wasting away of such a kind and brilliant man and partly it was; it breaks my heart just to think of John sometimes. But it was also so much fun to talk with him. I could be quick when he wasn't, I could be witty and give him a hard time, and even though he couldn't respond at my speed or with the agility of his youth, he understood that I was joking, and he loved it. I could see the spark in his eyes. It felt to me as if every funny remark he did manage—even if he had unknowingly made the same joke just a few moments before—was an expression of his gratitude to me for being there and treating him like the man he actually was, and not the condition that dominated him in his final years. What was even more touching, and more heartbreaking, was that John knew exactly what had happened to him and willingly assented to the care that his state demanded. I remember once exiting an elevator with him. He turned to the left toward his room and then looked back at me and said, "I think my room is down here." I nodded and said, "Yes, it's the last one on the right." Before he walked away, he turned back to me with a huge grin that spoke clearly: *I know that was a stupid question, but I really did need your help, so I asked anyway.* Like Hannah, John accepted his own brokenness and asked for what he needed; and into John's brokenness, too, the Lord brought cause for joy.

If I ever lose my mind to dementia or Alzheimer's, I hope I end up like John. John, indeed, reveals a profound truth about suffering and dependence that is at the very heart of the problems the kingdom of Israel experienced. When Israel's kings tried to be like other monarchs, when they attempted to increase their power with no regard for laws and the worship of God, they were lost and their kingdoms began to crumble. In their lust for power and wealth, they lost sight of their fundamental dependence upon God: prosperity and good fortune has a way of affecting most of us that way. Thus, time and again, it took the crumbling of the kingdom or the onset of some particularly awful misfortune for Israel to turn back to God, because it was in those moments of suffering and pain that the Israelites would remember who brought them peace and fulfillment. The lesson was not that God wanted Israel to suffer, but rather that God did not stand apart from the suffering of his people. God meets us where we are and when we are ready to meet him, even if that place is somewhere where we think he ought to be absent.

What John understood as he approached his death in such reduced circumstances was that he was not in control of his own life; clearly this was not a realization that came upon him only in those final years. We tend to die much as we live. Somewhere over the course of his years, John undoubtedly realized that he depended on God completely, so when the time came that he could no longer even care for his bodily needs himself, it was not the shock it is for so many of us: John already knew who was in command. The grace of John's suffering was finding that the Lord did indeed care for him, did indeed find him when he was lost and led him to peace and joy. For most of us it takes being lost to realize how much we need God's guidance. We are the sheep that go astray whom God pursues individually; when we are found, we realize not just how much we need God, but how much God truly longs for us.

It is the story of the kingdom of Israel. The second king of Israel, David, was a man graced by God and particularly talented. He was undoubtedly charismatic and apparently a good general and administrator. As he saw his kingdom flourishing around him, he was not unmindful of God, at least not at first. Indeed, he desired to build God a great temple that would last for all ages. But herein lay the problem: David wanted to build God's kingdom, instead of recognizing that it was God who had built David's kingdom. So when David proposed to the prophet Nathan that he build a house for God, God told Nathan to stop David from proceeding with his plan. Instead, God promised that he would make David's kingdom last for all ages. With the gift of hindsight it is so obvious what God was telling David: you depend on me, not I on you, because palaces and temples pass away, but God's promises last forever. Yet even in this gentle reprimand of David, God promised to be with David and his people, but in God's way, not David's.

Anointing

I said, *I wouldn't presume,*
Which is good,
Because I ought not to,
Since it's you, and, well—

Let's just not forget
That you were laughing
When you asked me to come,
Not at me or the prospect,
But playfully—*hilariously*—

So whenever I think
I'm about to have it figured,
I need only remember

That certainty is not the goal,
And I should only be sure
That you lead me—

And then laugh,
Deeply, as only the broken
Laugh when they're healed.

Fifteenth Meditation: David's Sin

Nathan said to David, "You are the man! Thus says the
LORD, the God of Israel: I anointed you king over Israel, and
I rescued you from the hand of Saul; I gave you your master's
house, and your master's wives into your bosom, and gave you
the house of Israel and of Judah; and if that had been too
little, I would have added as much more. Why have you
despised the word of the LORD, to do what is evil in his sight?
You have struck down Uriah the Hittite with the sword, and
have taken his wife to be your wife, and have killed him with
the sword of the Ammonites."

—2 Samuel 12:7–9

In the story of God's relationship with David, there is a clear sense
that God particularly favored and loved David. God's favoritism
when it came to David is, I think, somewhat confounding to us.
Not only does it grate against our understanding of God's equal
love for all his children, but even if it were fair that the Lord

would single out one man to love more than others, David seems hardly the appropriate choice. For when we think of David, we always remember Bathsheba. The entire story of their courtship is unsavory and disconcerting. It begins with David spying on her while she bathes and only gets worse from there. David abuses the power of his office to force her to sleep with him even though she is already married and then, in the most despicable moment of all, insures that her husband is slaughtered in battle to solve the problem of her pregnancy with his child. Yet we assume too much if we take God's favoritism regarding David literally. Certainly, God loved David in a particular and passionate way, but that is not what made God's love of David unique: that is how God loves all people. Rather, if David was God's favorite, then two things become evident about their relationship: that God expected much of David and that David was especially in need of God's love.

As a mother shows special attention to whichever of her children is suffering most, God singled out David because David was a sinner, not in spite of the fact. At the same time, God knew what David was capable of and so did not hesitate to request much of him, knowing that this man could do great things for the people of Israel. The lesson that David continually needed to relearn was how to live fully in God's presence. His life was one that constantly vacillated between piety and pride, between faith and arrogance, between focusing on the Lord whose prophet anointed him king and focusing on the kingdom he inordinately loved to rule. Yet every time he wandered, God called David back into his presence. For God delighted in David's presence.

The delight of the Lord was particularly evident in the life of another Jesuit, one I'll call Richard. Perhaps in part it was because, like David, Richard especially needed God's love in those final months of his life. Of all the men whose minds suffered from dementia at Sacred Heart, there was no one further along than Richard was. On his best days, he was capable of simple conversations; once I was even able to hear a little about where he grew up. Mostly, though, Richard was not capable of normal interaction, and when he could speak, it was only a few words about whatever was on his mind, and hardly ever in response to what was spoken to him. Richard was, in this state, nearly always frustrated. I didn't need anyone to tell me what almost everyone did: that Richard had been a meticulous person in his active life, and, while he was incredibly kind, he was also demanding. It was obvious that this was who he had been, because it was who he remained. So his consternation was considerable because he rarely knew what was going on around him, or where he was supposed to be; still less did he quietly suffer his own inability to care for himself. On a typical day, when I would walk by his slightly open bedroom door I'd hear him calling out to the nurses that he needed to get up now. I quickly learned that, for the most part, the nurses had to ignore his demands, simply because he always wanted to be up. All of this coupled with his wasted frame and constantly pained facial expression could have left me disgusted or terrified by Richard, or perhaps I might have pitied him. But God loved him too well for me to think of him in those terms.

It was a Friday morning, and it had been a long week. Indeed, I desperately wanted to get away from Sacred Heart that morning, frustrated with a few of the people I served in particular, and exhausted from the emotional and spiritual strain of my work. I was unsure whether I wanted more to scream or to collapse onto my bed and cry. I was doing my best to solider through, for it was only one more day until my day off. As I walked by Richard's room that morning, I heard him calling out "help" over and over. I would often go into his room when I heard him; I had the time to spend with him the nurses did not, so I liked to see if I could calm him down by speaking with him. I walked in and found him sitting in his wheelchair. He looked up at me expectantly as I entered, and beckoned to me. I crouched down by him and asked what he needed. Our conversation, as it turned out, was about breakfast. He thought that the way we did breakfast at Sacred Heart was all wrong, and at my prompting, he explained how breakfast ought to be served. He went over it with me a couple of times and then asked if I could do something about it; I told him that I thought I could talk to someone. This satisfied him, and after only another minute or so, I left his room. Our conversation, if it is not already obvious, was meaningless: indeed, the way of serving breakfast he described was nothing more than the very way breakfast had been served to him that morning. But something much more profound had passed between us than those inane words. For as I left Richard, I was completely cured of my melancholy: I was still tired and looking forward to Saturday, but I was curiously at ease and prepared to work for the rest of the day. I knew why, for it had not been Richard alone whom I had encountered in that room: Christ had been with him, and the consoling peace of the Lord had swept over my heart as we spoke.

King David, of course, did not know Christ as Richard did, but what Richard taught me that day was exactly the lesson David spent his whole life learning. Richard knew how to dwell in God's presence, through sinfulness and delight, through the mundane and the sublime, through breakfast and my melancholy. Being with God had become easy for Richard: he had spent his whole life oriented toward the service of the Lord and trying to bring himself wholly into God's presence; in those final years, it seemed as if he was just about there. He was still stubborn and frustrated, he was still suffering, but God was with him throughout it all. There was such goodness, such gentleness and love in Richard; I delighted to be with him. God's love of Richard, and Richard's unflinching response, overwhelmed me; it was so beautiful. Richard, like David, was one of God's favorites. In those painful last months, Richard really needed the Lord, just as David had in his sinfulness. And so, too, God expected much of Richard, because Richard was capable of so much: even as he died, Richard was still proclaiming the gospel to me, and who knows how many others. For God was with him.

God's Delight

When David was God's favorite,
He was arrogant, an ingrate,
Who squandered wit and charm
On the pleasures of state.

And I asked the Lord
About that once,
Wondering how it felt
To see David after he'd
Crushed so many hopes,
After he'd turned love
To profit.

I won't say
That God was confused,
But he looked at me
So quizzically
That I asked again,
What it felt like *after*,
When David came to him.

Which is when the Lord spoke
Of delight, of a heart coursing
With joy, brimming over
With laughter's nectar,

And I realized—
In no way I can comprehend—

That it was David God wanted,
Not the ruler or the penitent,
Not the adulterer or the magnificent,
Not the one he tried to be

But the one he was
When he was honestly
With the Lord.

Sixteenth Meditation:
The Covenant with David

*Your house and your kingdom shall be made sure forever
before me; your throne shall be established forever.*
—2 Samuel 7:16

The great irony of the short-lived glory of Israel was that it was
never that glorious. Israel was forever trying to find its way back
to peace and security, and its glories usually came, not from its
own efforts, but from God's direct intervention. When the
Israelites wanted a king—so that they could be powerful like
other nations—God gave them a king, even though God had
made clear that they needed no king but himself. But God
granted them a whole line of kings, and used their selfish request
to create with them a new covenant, a promise of a different sort
of kingdom. For it was from the house of David that Christ came:
that God himself came as the new king of Israel, just as God had
intended to be in the beginning. Then there were the prophets,
who sought after Israel each time Israel wandered away from
God. When Israel's own sinfulness led them into periods of great
suffering, God loved Israel so much that he sent them wondrous

and loving men to lead them back home. In the darkness of Israel's self-imposed suffering, God gave them more light than they had had before they had turned away. Yet the light of God is not always easy to find amid suffering, as prophets like Jeremiah, who was more often hated and plotted against than listened to, can attest. At Sacred Heart, I found tremendous suffering, evidence of the sinful world where we live, and that suffering broke my heart continually. It hardly mattered whether the man who suffered was harming himself by his attitude or whether he was completely innocent: these were good men whom I loved, and I hated to see them suffering. Yet I loved to find light in their eyes amid that suffering, and the light I did find was tremendous and moving. As with Israel, so with Sacred Heart: God's love was mysteriously more evident where it should have been entirely absent.

I could tell that they were all dying, some slowly and some with shocking rapidity. As my weeks passed with them, I found out about some of work they had done over the course of their lives. To say that many of them had had impressive ministerial careers would be a grave understatement: nearly all of them had done truly amazing work in the Lord's service. But that wasn't what I saw most of the time, and I didn't really need to see it. I saw who they were, and I saw their struggles; I saw their faith and their doubts, their senses of humor and their compassion. The kingdom of Israel passed away because that is in the nature of kingdoms. The men with whom I lived and worked at Sacred Heart had not become Jesuits in order to build up earthly kingdoms. Neither did God make promises to Israel in an attempt to create the world's first superpower. Rather, God's love is quite unlike what we expect; it reveals itself in powerlessness and suffering more often than it does in the schemes of the ambitious. It was in dying that the men at Sacred Heart taught me about how God loves.

Fond of Love

> We're fond of saying that love
> Gets complicated
> Like a spider's web we walk through
> And find pieces of clinging to us all day,
>
> But it's not really.
> It's not even like liking strawberry jelly
> When sometimes it seems divine
> And sometimes we crave it, lacking,
> Or curse the way it gets all over
> And falsely swear we've had enough.
>
> No. Love is, love is,
> Love is emptying you—
> If only a little at first—
> To pour into the waiting heart,
> The waiting arms, the waiting earth
> That longs to be filled.
>
> *Fear is like a labyrinth,*
> *Doubt is pure confusion,*
> *Hatred, an unsolvable puzzle,*
> But love—
>
> Love is dying
> To give life.

For Further Reflection

Prelude

2 Samuel 7:12–14a

What securities in your life are most important to you? Where is God in these securities?

Thirteenth Meditation: Hannah

1 Samuel 1:1–8   Hannah and Elkanah

1 Samuel 1:9–19a   Hannah's Request for a Son

1 Samuel 1:19b—2:11   Samuel Is Born and Offered to the Lord

What resentments do you struggle most to bring before God? How can you approach the Lord about these things?

Fourteenth Meditation: King David

1 Samuel 8:1–9   Israel Demands a King

1 Samuel 16:1–13   Samuel Anoints David King of Israel

What broken places in your life do you most need the Lord to anoint and make whole?

Fifteenth Meditation: David's Sin

2 Samuel 11:1–27   David's Sin (Bathsheba)

2 Samuel 12:1–25   David's Repentance

Recall a time when you, like David, have come before the Lord contrite. How did the Lord respond to your repentance?

Sixteenth Meditation: The Covenant with David

2 Samuel 7:1–17   David's Desire to Build a Temple and the Davidic Covenant

What love in your life is least complicated? Why is it so simple?

VI

Upon Their Hearts

Prelude

*No longer shall they teach one another, or say to each other,
"Know the Lord," for they shall all know me, from the least of
them to the greatest, says the Lord; for I will forgive their
iniquity, and remember their sin no more.*

—Jeremiah 31:34

Covenant of Hearts

It seems that love and death
Both depend on the condition
Of a heart that beats, whether
Rapidly or fleetingly, skipping
Or ceasing, in the end, to beat,

But always so significantly
In our emotion and physicality,
Always serving to remind us
Of the life that we have lived
Suffering, longing, and loving.

So when Jeremiah promised us
That your new covenant would
Be written on our hearts then

We knew that our lives would
Not follow the usual plot,

As life hasn't since the first
Heart forsook its own rhythm
To listen for you, to be loved
By the one who makes hearts,
And whose heart broke for us.

Seventeenth Meditation:
The Babylonian Exile

*They burned the house of God, broke down the wall of
Jerusalem, burned all its palaces with fire, and destroyed all its
precious vessels. He took into exile in Babylon those who had
escaped from the sword, and they became servants to him and
to his sons until the establishment of the kingdom of Persia.*
—2 Chronicles 36:19–20

I haven't always thought of the ocean as a cure for what ails me.
I've always loved the ocean, though being a naturalized northern
Californian, I prefer cold, rocky beaches to the warm and sandy
variety. But before Santa Barbara, I had never thought of any
beach as the place to nurse my wounds. So when I found myself
feeling lost and broken at the start of my second quarter at UC
Santa Barbara, I didn't start walking beside the ocean because I
expected the sea to soothe me. Having just ended a destructive
friendship in which I had already enabled my friend's harmful
behavior too long, I found myself suddenly very lonely, with considerable time on my hands in which to realize how deeply I had
been wounded in my effort to save someone who didn't want to

be saved. So I walked, which was natural enough for me, and since I lived by the ocean, I walked by the ocean. Soon I was walking two or three hours a day, always along the same route along the cliffs, past the edge of campus, and down to the Goleta Pier, where I would sit and stare at the ocean for awhile before turning back. I know I walked at all hours of the day then, but I remember most vividly the night walks. It was where the story began: before the ocean held any particular significance for me, I was very conscience of the night. It was a dark time in my life, and so in the beginning there was only one thing I knew how to do: I let the night be the night. That gave the Lord a place to begin.

No single book of the Old Testament chronicles the Babylonian captivity. Several have accounts of the conquest of Israel by King Nebuchadnezzar of Babylon, but perhaps even more significantly, the cataclysmic impact upon the consciousness of Israel is evident throughout books in which the captivity is never mentioned. Indeed, scholars suggest that many of the Old Testament books were compiled and revised while the Jewish elite class was held captive in Babylon. Scholarly and historical examinations belong to a different sort of book, yet to bring up this much is relevant for a simple reason: the destruction of the temple, the toppling of the kingdom, and the exile of the ruling class was of no little significance in the life of Israel. The Old Testament leaves us with little doubt that to many who experienced it, the Babylonian conquest of Israel felt as if all the promises God had made long ago had suddenly come to nothing. This was not how the Lord was supposed to treat his special possession. The world became very dark for Israel.

But in that dark there were voices. Prophets like Jeremiah and Isaiah, who had tried to warn Israel of where their wickedness and pride would lead, suddenly sounded like the mouthpieces of God to the very people who had derided their prophecies as treasonous blasphemy. The strange stories of Ezekiel, told during the

Exile, spoke of the hope that God would build something still greater from the rubble of the kingdom. And the poets began to sing a new sort of song. Of all the literature composed about the Exile, there is perhaps none so hauntingly evocative as Psalm 137, which begins, "By the rivers of Babylon—there we sat down and there we wept when we remembered Zion." Its simple elegance addresses the problem of the Exile boldly. The psalmist speaks of being asked by his captors in Babylon to sing one of the old festive melodies of Israel—a song, perhaps, of God's triumph over the Egyptians, or of the glories of Jerusalem when King David danced and prayed before the Ark of the Covenant. How, the poet asks, could he sing of the glories of Israel while an exile in a foreign land? The psalm never curses God, saving its vitriol for Israel's captors, but the anger of the psalmist is such that I wonder what he thought about God in that moment. Certainly, he wanted the Lord to come and slaughter his enemies, to show the conquerors of Israel who the Lord God of Hosts was, but the psalm leaves lingering questions. I wonder if the author felt that it was no time to praise the Lord because he could no longer find any reason to praise God.

The transformation that came upon Israel in Babylon reminds me of the ocean. In the bitter depths of abandonment and pain, Israel learned to sing new songs to the Lord: they learned to love the Lord anew, and to think about their relationship with God in ways they never had during times of prosperity. They came to depend upon God and found that dependence more wonderful than all the glories of the kingdom. It wasn't long after my walks down to the Goleta Pier began that I found myself one night staring out into the black expanse of the ocean. I was very lonely that night, as I had been for some time. It was not just my friends and family I missed, but the Lord. I didn't understand how it had come to that, but it had. My faith had all but slipped away, and I hadn't really even noticed that it had. All I knew that night was that I didn't know how to talk to God anymore. Just months before I had defined my identity by my faith, and yet somehow in my effort to do a good thing—to help my friend get away from her self-destructive behavior with alcohol and drugs—everything had become hazy for me. I hated Santa Barbara: I hated the university and the hedonistic culture that pervaded it, and I hated everything about this foreign place so far from the home where I had sung of the glories of the Lord with passion and skill. Something in the ocean captured me that night. As I looked out into the waves, I suddenly felt as if I were somewhere else entirely, that I was utterly alone, although the pier was full of other people. It was the most profound loneliness, and yet there was something else in it: something good and hopeful, something holy. I thought to myself that *I don't think I ever believed the waves had this look in them* and quickly pulled a piece of paper and pen out of my pocket. I didn't quite understand it yet, but I wrote it. I poured my heart out onto paper without quite realizing what I was saying: that in the loneliness of that night on the pier, I had found the Lord after all.

I came back to the ocean again and again after that. Everything looked different when I walked and sat by the sea. It was never an escape, for I could not come without my own injured spirit. When I looked out into the ocean, I saw it through my own fatigue and suffering. In the verses that suddenly began to pour from my lips and onto page after page, I cast all of my cares out onto those waves. I began to pray honestly, perhaps more honestly than I had ever prayed. And instead of responding to my bitterness and self-absorption with rebuke or silence, the Lord took each accusation, each plea and cry, and turned it into something beautiful. I gathered the worst of the world and myself into my hands and offered it to God on those shores, and yet I always walked back to my dorm room more hopeful. I wrote like I had never written before, and it was indeed *better* than it had ever been—that was certainly God's gift to me, for it encouraged me to keep writing. But more than just being better, there was a vulnerable honesty in my words that I never knew I was capable of. I spoke from the deepest parts of my heart and I found, in those depths, not only my brokenness, but the Lord waiting for me with a new promise of being whole.

The Exile was, in some ways, only the beginning of Israel's troubles. Doubtless, when King Cyrus of Persia returned the Jewish elites to Israel and the kingdom was restored, it felt as if God had finally heard the pleas of his people and would soon restore Israel to glory. It is indeed Cyrus who is first called a messiah—the anointed savior of Israel—in the Old Testament. Yet as much as Israel was able to rebuild after the return from the Exile, the restoration of the kingdom of David and Solomon never really happened. After the Persians, the Greeks conquered Israel and after the Greeks came the Romans. The kings of Israel spoken of in the gospels, indeed, are little more than the puppets of Rome, and certainly not descended from David's line. The Babylonian captivity, like the Exodus before it, had forever changed the history of Israel, except this time it didn't make any sense. After the Exodus, Israel had become God's people, been given the laws that defined it, and had inherited a land and kingdom that seemed to fulfill all of their longings. After the Exile, it seemed as if Israel could never be that kingdom again.

Yet at the very moment when everything was on the verge of collapse, when the last kings of David's line were ignoring the Lord and his prophets in their headlong pitch toward the Exile, the fact that Israel's kingdom would never be the same was precisely what God had tried to tell them. The prophet Jeremiah was hated, perhaps the most hated of all Israel's prophets. In my experience, the book of Jeremiah is a thoroughly depressing, incredibly moving, and unmistakably hopeful work. Yet my own contradictory emotions journeying with Jeremiah must be no more than the merest shadow of the confusion that raged within Jeremiah as he lived out his public ministry. At one point,

Jeremiah reflects upon why he keeps preaching disaster to an angry and unwilling audience and realizes that "within me there is something like a burning fire…I am weary with holding it in, and I cannot" (Jer 20:9). His love for the Lord and his faith in the Lord's word felt like so much trickery when he realized the suffering it brought him, yet he could not bring himself to stop doing as the Lord asked: he loved God too much for that. It was this man, this hated and long-suffering servant of the Lord, who told Israel of God's new covenant.

Perhaps it was a promise that only made sense to the broken. Certainly few paid Jeremiah's prophecy much attention while he was alive. It was at once something entirely new and completely familiar. God said again that he would be Israel's God, that the Israelites would be his people. Yet this covenant would not be written on stone tablets, but on the very hearts of the people. Stone could be broken, ignored, locked away. This law would become part of who God's people were, and "no longer shall they teach one another, or say to each other, 'Know the Lord' for they shall all know me, from the least of them to the greatest" (Jer 31:34). For all the beauty of the promise, God was no longer pledging to make Israel a great nation. The Lord promised that he would never again forsake his people, and even spoke of a glorious new Jerusalem, but a covenant of hearts was not about kingdoms: it was about a relationship. It was the relationship that had been at the center of every covenant, but this time there would be no intermediary: no ark, no land, no mountain, no temple. God would meet his people in the very flesh of their hearts. The Lord was preparing to enter into the hearts that had broken when Babylon conquered Israel.

I shed many tears on the Goleta Pier. I ached on the Santa Barbara shore and felt pain such as I had never felt before. I never want to go back to that suffering, but I go back to that sea nearly every time I put pen to paper, because it was by that ocean that the

Lord taught me how to write, as if I had never written before. I came to depend upon God there—or rather, I came to understand how much I had always depended on him. In all of my successes as a student and as a church minister, I had made the same mistake that Israel made: in my prosperity, I had forgotten who makes us prosperous. But by that ocean, I found my way back to God through the very brokenness that separated me from the Lord. In the honest humility of my poems, I discovered not the means to bolster my sagging ego but a place where I could meet the Lord without pretension, in the simplicity of one heart open to another.

Forlorn Ocean

I don't think I ever believed
The waves had this look in them,
Or that a pier could be so far from land.
And I wasn't even quite alone:
Somewhere on the wooden planks
There were fishermen,
And strolling lovers,
And strollers who were not lovers,
And none of them probably far from me,
But as I stared out into the darkness,
Into the vastness of the sea,
Something overwhelming took hold
And all I could feel was alone.

As tears that would not come prickled,
My weary heart cried out a sinking song—
Some sort of longing to be lost
In that loneliness—
And just before I turned back to land
And bright light and sidewalks
I wondered where that loneliness would take me.

And something reminded me of

A bridge, a gap, the beginning
Of where you're always waiting to meet me
Somewhere in the depths
Of my water-logged,
Or your water-logged, soul.

Sometimes I have to remind myself
That I believe
In the forlornness of the ocean
And the end of being alone.

Eighteenth Meditation: Zechariah

Zechariah said to the angel, "How will I know that this is so?
For I am an old man, and my wife is getting on in years."
The angel replied, "I am Gabriel. I stand in the presence of
God, and I have been sent to speak to you and to bring you
this good news."

—Luke 1:18–19

It was with just a few open hearts that God began again, just as
God had always begun. The Gospel of Luke is particularly insis-
tent upon this point: no matter how new the covenant, the Lord
was still the Lord, God of Israel. And Zechariah was nothing if not
an Israelite. The story is familiar in many ways: the angel Gabriel
came to Zechariah, a priest of the temple, to tell him that
although he and his wife Elizabeth were old and childless, they
would nevertheless have a son who would find favor in the sight
of the Lord. Zechariah's reaction is not dissimilar to that of

Abraham and Sarah when they were given the same news: he doesn't believe it, and has the audacity to say so to the angel Gabriel. It is tempting to condemn Zechariah for his unbelief— if he recognized that he was speaking to an angel, surely he could accept the word of an angel. Or perhaps we might bristle at the harsh reaction of Gabriel: upon hearing Zechariah's protests, he makes him mute until, after his son is born, he comes around and acquiesces to God's plan. It is a puzzling encounter, even more so when we realize that until the moment Gabriel silences Zechariah, their exchange effectively followed the script of covenant conversations. Yet Gabriel knew what Zechariah needed nine months to understand: this was an offer made not to the proud-hearted, not to the ambitious or the powerful, but to the suffering and the broken. God was not coming on Israel's terms, but on God's own; this time when they demanded a king, God would insist that there was to be no king but the Lord himself. Zechariah was a good and faithful servant of the Lord; his heart, in the end, was open to what the Lord proposed. It took the brokenness and shame of his enforced silence for Zechariah to recognize where the Lord was present.

When I graduated from UC Santa Barbara, I never meant to return. It wasn't something I consciously admitted, but when I went there on my Jesuit pilgrimage, it was the first thing I realized. As the Greyhound bus I took from Los Angeles to Santa Barbara got closer and I began to recognize familiar sights, my stomach began to knot. But then, as I caught my first glimpse of the Santa Barbara ocean, the realization swept over me in an icy wave: I had intended to stay away from that ocean for the rest of my life. Other oceans were wonderful: I could walk in Monterey, or write poems in Los Angeles, or even watch whales in Uruguay, and all I would think of was how much I loved the ocean and even how many ways the Lord had been kind and gracious to me by the sea in Santa Barbara. It was a delightful memory, a place to which I willingly returned in poems. But actually setting foot again upon that pier, actually looking out into those waves, was a different matter. I am as good as anyone at pretending that I am not broken, which is to say that I try very hard but am no good at the pretense at all. Zechariah knew that Gabriel had come to answer his prayers and the prayers of all God's chosen people: he knew that this was it, and the Lord was coming. But to meet the Lord meant to admit just how broken he was, to acknowledge that Israel was no longer a land flowing with milk and honey but a place of pain and frustration.

The Lord would not suffer any pretense, from Zechariah or from me. So I returned to the ocean in Santa Barbara. A year later, I found myself by the same ocean, but this time in Honolulu. Almost everything about that shore, from the sand and the water to the sky, proclaimed that this was a place unique and entirely apart. This beach ought not to have reminded me of Santa Barbara, but as I walked along the Ala Moana beach on a sunny Friday afternoon, I knew that I was once more at God's ocean. I was thinking of so many things in that moment, of troubles past and present, of Monterey, and Santa Barbara, and the San Francisco Bay, of brokenness and the promises of the Lord. I realized on that day—for perhaps the thousandth time—that there was no place to hide from God at the ocean. Yet I had no desire to hide from God. As much as the Lord complicates my life, and leads me places I would not go of my own accord, my broken heart open to the Lord is more full than the proud heart I bear when I pretend that I am self-sufficient. Sometimes it takes an ocean to remind me of that.

Out of Silence

A man gets used to talking,
To saying, to explaining,
And certainly when they
Are always asking and expecting

It's easy to let words
Run away with sense,
To forget entirely
The sanctity of silence—

Which is no excuse
For talking back to an angel,
For affronting Gabriel
With boundless ego.

But still Zechariah was not
Hopeless, not a man bent
On twisting God's will
Into a more pleasing form:

He just wouldn't shut up,
Wouldn't listen to God talking,
Wouldn't see the glory brimming
Over in the very air before him.

So the Lord's angel smiled
And told him to be quiet,
With all the subtlety
Of Godly familiarity,

So that Zechariah could find
The holiness of the silence,
And hear good reason
To speak again.

Nineteenth Meditation: Elizabeth

After those days his wife Elizabeth conceived, and for five
months she remained in seclusion. She said, "This is what the
Lord has done for me when he looked favorably on me and
took away the disgrace I have endured among my people."

—Luke 1:24–25

For Elizabeth, it took Mary to be reminded of her dependence
upon God. Elizabeth, the wife of Zechariah, didn't know what
had taken place in the temple between Gabriel and her husband.
She knew that *something* had happened, just as everyone did when
he emerged mute. But it must have troubled her even more than
her husband's muteness when she realized, weeks later, that she
was pregnant. This, she knew, could only have been the work of
the Lord, and I don't think it is a great leap to suppose that
Elizabeth assumed her pregnancy had something to do with
whatever had silenced her husband. Her reaction testifies to her
mystification: recognizing the Lord's hand at work, but uncertain
as to the meaning of what was now occurring, she retreated into
solitude for five months. It is a credit to Elizabeth's faith that she
so willingly believed that her ability to conceive was the work of
the Lord, and not terribly damning that she wasn't sure how to
cope with this new reality. God's angel never appeared to
Elizabeth to explain matters, and yet there was so obviously something afoot, and Elizabeth did not know how she could possibly
have any role to play in God's new scheme. But Mary changed
everything for Elizabeth, for when she caught sight of Mary,
Elizabeth recognized the Lord's presence more clearly than if she
had seen whole hosts of angelic choirs arrayed before her. In this
younger woman coming to visit her, Elizabeth saw God at work
and began to believe in the promise of the new covenant.

The encounter is remarkable for its ordinariness. Mary has
seen the angel Gabriel and been told that she will have a son

through the power of the Holy Spirit, but Elizabeth did not know this, just as she did not know that Gabriel had also appeared to her husband. All Elizabeth saw was Mary, and yet that was enough. At the sound of Mary's voice, and perhaps with the merest glance at her, Elizabeth knew that this was the mother of the Lord. The gospel writer gives only a passing explanation for why: when Elizabeth heard Mary's greeting, her child leapt within her womb. And yet Elizabeth seemed to know everything: she knew that Mary was pregnant, that she was the mother of the Lord, that God had been able to work in Mary because she "believed that there would be a fulfillment of what was spoken to her by the Lord" (Luke 1:45). Noah witnessed the destruction of most of the world. Abraham heard an angel yelling for him to stop before he killed his son. Moses saw a bush that burned but was not consumed, and dozens of other wonders. David built a kingdom on the promise of the Lord. And Elizabeth saw Mary. I don't know what made it all so clear in Elizabeth's mind, and I doubt that she could have explained what she suddenly knew—indeed, she said to Mary that she still did not understand why God would involve her in his plans. But God spoke to her in those moments, and everything was changed.

Elizabeth

From the beginning
You knew God was up to something
And that was terrifying, exciting,
Mesmerising, surprising,
And God knows what else,

And that was it, of course—
God knew every bit of what and why,
And you didn't, so you just
Wanted time to think

To feel a dozen different ways,
To be awestruck, disbelieving.

But when Mary came
You knew the Lord
As no angel in majesty,
No messenger of heaven
Could explain:

This woman, your cousin,
Who suddenly seemed so young,
Was the mother of the Lord,

And that was no answer,
No solution to confusion,
No explanation for why
You had anything to do with it—

But you knew
And your heart
Leapt with the infant
In your womb,

For this was the beginning
You were caught up in.

Twentieth Meditation: The New Covenant

The days are surely coming, says the LORD, when I will make a new covenant with the house of Israel and the house of Judah. It

*will not be like the covenant that I made with their ancestors
when I took them by the hand to bring them out of the land of
Egypt—a covenant that they broke, though I was their husband,
says the LORD. But this is the covenant that I will make with
the house of Israel after those days, says the LORD: I will put
my law within them, and I will write it on their hearts; and I
will be their God, and they shall be my people.*

—Jeremiah 31:31–33

Perhaps it was a word that only the humbled could understand.
The ocean, for all its vastness, for all its enchantment and beauty,
is only the ocean. The Lord has yet to appear to me on the shore
and explain it all. I've spoken to God by the ocean dozens of
times, but in ordinary, not miraculous, ways. I met God at the sea
in those months in Santa Barbara because I was ready to meet
him; he had merely been waiting for the opportunity. When I
came to the ocean, I did not hide that I was broken, I did not pretend that I didn't need the Lord: I needed God to heal me, and I
told him that, by being no less angry and upset, no less wounded
and confused, no less hopeful and vulnerable than I actually was.
So the Lord came into the gaping place I had left open in my
heart. It was a familiar story, for the Lord had come that way to
Zechariah, Elizabeth, and Mary. Mary may have always been open
to the Lord, while Elizabeth needed some persuading, and
Zechariah more drastic measures, but all of them were children of
Israel, confused and longing for the God who they knew loved
Israel, but whose presence was hard to discern in such a broken
land. They were ready for God, so God came to dwell among his
people in the son of Mary, Jesus.

The Lord has asked many things of me by the ocean, and usually it begins not with God carefully laying out his proposals, but
with the simple question: *Will you?* To my great consternation,
there is often little else, and I do not know what it is the Lord is

asking of me before I have to decide whether to say yes. But as much as I might complain that Mary had an angel who explained it all, I know that it is not so simple. For Mary had no idea what she was beginning—no matter the explanations the Lord provides, when God asks us to go beyond ourselves and enter into his life and work, we are being asked to embrace the unknown. The prospect is terrifying, and yet God promises to be with us, and so, time and again, we say yes, because being with God is well worth the uncertainty. God's invitation is always one in which he asks us to trust him, to rest assured that we will be his people and he will be our God. The assenting voices of God's people over the history of Israel inspire and challenge us to love God more deeply, just as they also reassure us that God can forgive even impertinent sinners such as ourselves. Perhaps even more so, they reassure us that God's love is always particular, always of specific people, always given in a manner that suits the moment. We need only say yes.

I Say Yes to God

First you said,
Let's sail into uncharted waters
Without so much as a compass
And I hesitatingly said,
Well, as long as you're there.

Then you said,
Lose the life-preserver
And cut the anchor,
And I said,
If you say so.

Then you said,
Abandon the ship
For the lifeboat

And forget the oars.
And I said,
All right.

Then, just this morning, you said,
Let go of the rudder,
Sit easy and smile,
And don't worry about knowing
Where we're going, because I do.
And I said,
Yes.

For Further Reflection

Prelude

Jeremiah 31:34

When have you "forsaken your own rhythm" to enter into the love and life of another? What did this entail?

Seventeenth Meditation: The Babylonian Exile

Isaiah 5:1–7   The Prophecy Regarding the Fall of Israel

Jeremiah 26:1–15   Jeremiah Is Threatened with Death for His Prophecies

Jeremiah 34:1–22   The Fall of Jerusalem

2 Kings 24:8–17   The Fall of Jerusalem

2 Chronicles 36:9–21   The Fall of Jerusalem

Psalm 137   The Babylonian Captivity

2 Chronicles 36:22–23   The Restoration by Cyrus, King of Persia

Ezra 1:1–11   The Restoration by Cyrus, King of Persia

Isaiah 40:1–11   The Promise of Comfort During the Babylonian Captivity

Ezekiel 37:1–14   The Promise of Restoration During the Babylonian Captivity

Has there ever been a "Babylon" in your life? What did you learn about yourself there? What did you learn about God there?

Eighteenth Meditation: Zechariah

Luke 1:5–23   Zechariah and Gabriel

What role does silence play in your life and prayer? Is it a good thing or a bad thing?

Nineteenth Meditation: Elizabeth

Luke 1:24–25   Elizabeth's Pregnancy

Luke 1:26–38   Mary and Gabriel

Luke 1:39–45   Mary and Elizabeth

Luke 1:57–80   The Birth of John the Baptist

Recall a time when you understood something in your heart long before you understood it in your mind. How did this understanding change your way of looking at the situation?

Twentieth Meditation: The New Covenant

Jeremiah 31:31–37   The Promise of the New Covenant

When is it easy to say yes to God? When is it most difficult?

Appendix: Connections to the Sunday Readings

The following tables suggest where individual meditations in this book have a connection to the readings for Sundays or holydays in the Catholic liturgical year. The table is intended to be a reference for anyone wishing to incorporate meditations from this book into Bible study, faith sharing, prayer groups, or personal reflection that is centered around the Sunday readings. Please note that not all meditations have a connection to the Sunday or holyday readings, and there are some meditations that are listed as being appropriate for multiple days.

The table is organized according to the liturgical year. The notation used here is that of the Catholic Lectionary. In addition to being available in any number of Catholic devotional magazines and pamphlets, the readings associated with each liturgical day are available on the U.S. Bishops' website (http://www.usccb. org/nab) and in the back of most Catholic Bibles.

Note: the abbreviation "OT" designates "Ordinary Time."

YEAR A

Lectionary Date	Biblical Topic	Meditation	Page
1st Sunday Lent	The Fall	Second	17
2nd Sunday Lent	Call of Abram	Fifth	33
3rd Sunday Lent	Water from the Rock	Twelfth	62
4th Sunday Lent	Samuel Anoints David	Fourteenth	73
5th Sunday Lent	Prophecy of Resurrection	Twentieth	101
11th Sunday OT	Covenant at Mt. Sinai	Prelude, Part 4	51
27th Sunday OT	Prophecy of Fall of Israel	Seventeenth	88

YEAR B

Lectionary Date	Biblical Topic	Meditation	Page
2nd Sunday Advent	Comfort for Israel	Seventeenth	88
4th Sunday Advent	Annunciation	Twentieth	101
Holy Family	Abraham's Covenant	Eighth	45
1st Sunday Lent	Noah's Covenant	Prelude, Part 2	13
2nd Sunday Lent	Sacrifice of Isaac	Seventh	40
4th Sunday Lent	Fall of Jerusalem	Seventeenth	88
5th Sunday Lent	New Covenant	Twentieth	101
10th Sunday OT	The Fall	Second	17
30th Sunday OT	Promise in Exile	Seventeenth	88

YEAR C

Lectionary Date	Biblical Topic	Meditation	Page
4th Sunday Advent	Visitation of Elizabeth	Nineteenth	99
Holy Family	Hannah Presents Samuel	Thirteenth	70
Baptism of the Lord	Comfort in Exile	Seventeenth	88
2nd Sunday Lent	Covenant with Abraham	Prelude, Part 3	32
3rd Sunday Lent	Burning Bush	Eleventh	58
11th Sunday OT	David and Bathsheba	Fifteenth	78
16th Sunday OT	Promise of Isaac	Sixth	30

ALL YEARS

Lectionary Date	Biblical Topic	Meditation	Page
Immaculate Conception	Annunciation	Twentieth	101
Immaculate Conception	Eve and the Fall (1st Reading)	Second	17
Annunciation	Annunciation (Gospel)	Twentieth	101
Easter Vigil	Creation (1st Reading)	First	14
Easter Vigil	Sacrifice of Isaac (2nd Reading)	Seventh	40
Easter Vigil	Red Sea (3rd Reading)	Twelfth	62
Assumption	Visitation of Elizabeth	Nineteenth	99

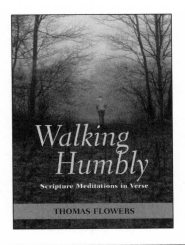

Walking Humbly
Scripture Meditations in Verse
Thomas Flowers

Through poetic reflections on familiar
scripture passages, *Walking Humbly* serves as a companion
to prayer for people seeking to draw closer to the
humanity and divinity of Jesus.

978-0-8091-4571-3
Paperback

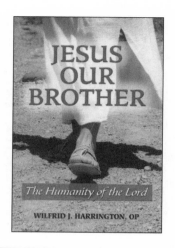

Jesus Our Brother
The Humanity of the Lord
Wilfrid J. Harrington, OP

A noted biblical scholar, revered teacher, and graceful
author writes movingly and with profound insight
about Jesus as human being.

978-0-8091-4671-0
Paperback

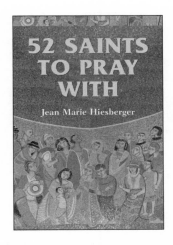

52 Saints to Pray With
Jean Marie Hiesberger

A brief presentation of fifty-two saints' lives with
reflections and practical ways to follow their
example in our own life and times.

978-0-8091-4648-2
Paperback

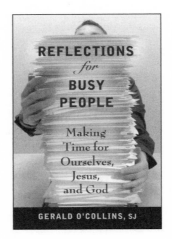

Reflections for Busy People

Making Time for Ourselves, Jesus, and God
Gerald O'Collins, SJ

This book provides accessible and manageable lines
of thought for busy people wishing to reflect
on the deeper realities of their lives.

978-0-8091-4606-2
Paperback

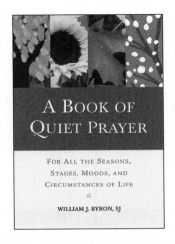

A Book of Quiet Prayer
For All the Seasons, Stages, Moods,
and Circumstances of Life
William J. Byron, SJ

Suggests ways and words for turning to God in faith, hope, and
love, in stages of life, in all imaginable circumstances.

0–8091–4362–3
Paperback

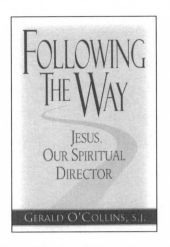

Following The Way
Jesus, Our Spiritual Director
Gerald O'Collins, SJ

World-renowned theologian Gerald O'Collins offers
a compelling book of spirituality, a beautifully written
examination of the parables for living them
in one's own life.

0-8091-3984-7
Paperback

Spiritual Masters for All Seasons
Michael Ford

HiddenSpring
Invites four spiritual masters onto the same stage for
the first time and shows how they speak—Thomas Merton,
Henri Nouwen, Anthony de Mello, and John O'Donahue—
while assessing their place in the world of
contemporary spirituality.

978-1-58768-055-7
Paperback

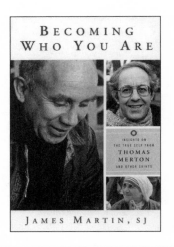

Becoming Who You Are
Insights on the True Self from
Thomas Merton and Other Saints
James Martin, SJ

By meditating on personal examples from the author's life,
as well as reflecting on the inspirational life and writings of
Thomas Merton, stories from the Gospels, as well as the lives
of other holy men and women (among them, Henri Nouwen,
Therese of Lisieux and Pope John XXIII) the reader
will see how becoming who you are, and becoming
the person that God created, is a simple path to
happiness, peace of mind and even sanctity.

1-58768-036-X
Paperback

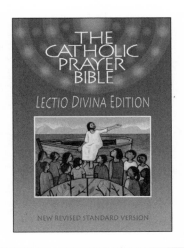

The Catholic Prayer Bible (NRSV)
Lectio Divina Edition
Paulist Press

An ideal Bible for anyone who desires to reflect on
the individual stories and chapters of just one, or even all,
of the biblical books, while being led to prayer
though meditation on that biblical passage.

978-0-8091-0587-8 Hardcover
978-0-8091-4663-5 Paperback